HOW TO HAVE A WEDDING AS INDIV

GU00937890

HOW TO HAVE A WEDDING AS INDIVIDUAL AS YOU ARE

ROSS WILLSHER

With love and thanks to

Mum & Dad
for being the best parents in the world

Maz & Ava
forever my favourite girls

&

James
for all of the adventures we have shared
and have yet to experience together

"To be yourself in a world that is constantly trying to make you something else is the greatest accomplishment."

Ralph Waldo Emerson

"I believe that photographs should be simple technically, and easy to look at. They shouldn't be directed at other photographers; their point is to make ordinary people react – to laugh, or to see something they hadn't taken in before, or to be touched..."

Lord Snowdon

"I've learned that people will forget what you said, people will forget what you did, but people will never forget how you made them feel."

Maya Angelou

Contents

Introduction

We've all had that experience at the hairdressers when, despite describing the exact style we are after (or even showing a photo), the stylist believes they know better and halfway through the session you suddenly realise you're not getting the cut you have asked for; it's already shorter, choppier and / or the wrong colour. However, you don't feel you can speak up at this point as the hairdresser is the expert and therefore they must know what they are doing. Who are you to advise them?

At the end of the session – when asked for feedback – you smile politely and say how lovely your hair looks, but you walk out of the salon feeling anything but yourself; annoyed at yourself for not speaking up and self-conscious that your hair is wearing you and not vice versa. Your hairdresser has styled your hair according to their own idea of how you should look and what is in vogue as opposed to what suits you and – more importantly – what you wanted.

This happens all the time with wedding planning too – you leave everything in the hands of the experts as they know far more than you do about all things wedding-related. However, they don't know you. You are the expert on yourself, your values, and how you want to celebrate the unique love that you have for one another. A bad haircut grows out after 4-5 awkward weeks – memories of a wedding that wasn't really you last forever.

I know full well what it is like to not be listened to; for people to make assumptions or believe they know what will suit me best. I also know what it is like to not have the confidence at times to always speak up when you feel uncomfortable. Expert advice is essential and should be heeded throughout the wedding planning process, but there is a huge difference between advice that is in your best interests and someone simply projecting their values onto you. This book is designed to help you feel empowered to design and create a wedding that is 100% true to you without bowing to other people's idea of what your special day should look like.

1

My Story

It has taken many many years for me to realise that being true to yourself and embracing your uniqueness is the greatest key to leading a happy and successful life. It has taken me just as long to understand that those that treat you negatively because of your willingness to be honest and open about who you are are quite often reacting to their own frustration at not being fully able to express themselves. We all need to feel free to live outside of the pigeon holes we are all too often placed in by our peers and the society we live in.

I feel strongly that we should be able to be ourselves and feel comfortable in our own skin at all times throughout our lives, but especially on our wedding day; the day we vow to spend the rest of our life with the person who loves us exactly the way we are.

For many years I was made to feel inferior and was treated negatively for behaviours or actions that made me appear different; I was never the kid with the coolest trainers or latest haircut. The fact I actually wanted to behave and listen to the teacher apparently made me perfect fodder for bullying, and spending my lunchtimes sat in the library not stood between the goalposts also seemed an indication that I was deserving of less favourable treatment from my classmates. Because I did not have the confidence to speak up for myself and share my stories and opinions without fear of ridicule, people would find humour in creating their own tales about who I was and what I believed in. Those lies and rumours led to assumptions being made and judgements being cast, before I even had the opportunity to show people the real me. Soon it became easier to lie low, keep quiet and hide anything that would lead to prejudice and mockery.

One of my strongest memories of Primary school is someone wiping their dirty tissue through my hair, and I look back at Secondary school and can still hear the laughter of my so-called friends as I was hit on the back of the head by a perfectly-aimed rucksack and called derogatory names on a daily basis. I realise looking back that the chances of me leaving the education system with a confidence and comfortableness in my own skin were slim to non-existent. Just as I was starting to look forward to life after school - a new college, the chance to go to university and meet a whole range of exciting people - I started to struggle with a new and scary realisation. A slow, steady, ever-strengthening feeling that my sexuality might be different to most of the population, and something that might isolate me further from certain sectors of mainstream society. I spent much of my late teenage years and early twenties agonising over a constant procession of anxiety-ridden questions. Why was this happening to me? How could I stop it? Hide it? Make sure no one found out about this – ever?! Was it my fault? Did it make me a bad person? For some, the realisation that they are gay is comforting and exciting and the desire to shout loudly and proudly about who they are feels undeniably natural, for others the agonising process of self-acceptance can last a lifetime. Sometimes, not being obviously effeminate or camp can count against a young gay man growing up. For me, people assuming I was straight often led to me hearing people's true prejudices and homophobia (whether casual changing room banter, or heartfelt confessions of hate). There were casual comments of "That's so gay" used to describe all manner of situations, items or activities that were deemed uncool or not worthy of somebody's time. There were older members of my local community who would call me a kind, thoughtful young lad in one breath and state their disgust at the latest celebrity to come out of the closet in their next. Experiences like these made me falsely believe it was easier to pretend to be what people thought I was, than to live an honest life that was true to who I was.

It took me until my early twenties to come out to my friends and family and to slowly and gently remove the layers of loneliness and fear of rejection that had restrictively woven around me for almost a decade. Luckily, my family (especially my wonderful parents and sister) and friends, were incredibly supportive and loving on learning of my sexuality and continue to be so. However, even after I was out to most people I still struggled a little with my own self-acceptance. I knew I was gay and so did my loved ones, but what did that mean and how would that influence my life?

Were there rules? Music I had to listen to? Clothes I had to wear? Behaviours I had to adopt? We've all heard at least a few gay stereotypes regarding the appearances, interests or behaviours of gay men or women. Slowly, over time, I realised that no – there are no rules to being gay. In fact, the more I realised this, the easier it was to be happy in my own skin and proud of who I was. That's not to say I actively avoided being a stereotype or that I pass judgement on anyone who happens to fit these stereotypes. I simply realised that being true to myself and my own values and beliefs is all that is necessary to be accepting and proud of who I am. My sexuality is no longer something I hide, nor something that defines how I live my life.

My experiences have made me passionate about embracing the unique qualities I have and valuing the one-of-a-kind personalities of others. In my personal and professional life, I strive to avoid making assumptions and preconceptions based on an individual's characteristics or appearance. All of us, in some way – however conscious or subconscious it may be – feel at times like we have to conform to certain behaviours and norms that relate to our gender, sexuality, faith, disability, physical appearance, skin colour or age.

A healthy exercise is to sit and question where this pressure to conform comes from and how our lives could improve by shaking off limiting beliefs about ourselves. Why I do think I am too old to learn a new skill? Who says I need to lose weight before I book that photoshoot?

By being myself, both in my job as a photographer and in my day to day life, I seek to inspire others to not only accept but celebrate who they are – as they are – without the need to change or bend to others' ideas of who they should be.

No Good Advice

When I started my business, lots of advice was offered from people both inside and outside of the industry. There were suggestions that I should keep my same sex relationship quiet in case potential clients – especially families with young children – would be put off by this.

I was informed I should reserve my online portfolio for the "beautiful couples" so as to only showcase my strongest images. Bizarrely, I was also told to "try and act" interested in each client to maximise the chances of them booking my services! (Surely if you aren't genuinely interested in the people seeking your services you shouldn't be in the profession?).

For the first few months of my business – mistakenly thinking that these experienced professionals knew best – I heeded their advice. I limited my portfolio to showcase couples with a certain look, I made sure my social media posts made no reference to my personal life and long term relationship and generally held part of my personality back for fear of it limiting my success. It felt wrong, it felt restrictive and it went against everything I believe in.

So I took the advice and flipped it completely on its head. I built a portfolio that centred on diversity and became open and honest about who I was. I realised that my ability to empathise with those who don't feel confident in who they are or don't fit easily into pigeon holes was my greatest strength. I stopped worrying about how other photographers used lighting, lenses and lustre print finishes and focused instead on how to make my clients feel comfortable in front of the camera.

Then, and only then, did my business begin to grow. I had clients who shared my values, who I enjoyed working with and who began to feel good about themselves.

"Well – that's a lovely story and approach to your business, Ross. I'm delighted for you, but what's all this got to do with my wedding?" I hear you say.

Well, weddings are incredibly precious events – often (hopefully) once in a lifetime – but they also come with stress and some anxiety. There are rules and traditions you feel you have to adhere to and pressure to plan your day the way you think it should be rather than how you would like it to be. You may feel conscious of not being like the couples you've seen in the wedding magazines – maybe because you are not as young, not as skinny or not marrying someone of the opposite sex. Social media may lead you to feel pushed into a certain style or theme, or you might want to be different and break the rules but not know how to start.

Some of this pressure to have a wedding that conforms to society's expectations comes from wedding suppliers themselves, and in a world where seemingly anything goes, there can appear to be very little out there to help couples plan a wedding that truly reflects who they are. It was during a recent visit to a wedding fair that this fact was really brought home to me.

The Other Side of the Supplier Stand

Recently, I attended a national wedding fair with a soon-to-be married friend. "Wahoo" I thought – a chance to visit a show without taking ten painstakingly embarrassing attempts to successfully construct my pop-up banner or weighing down the back of my car with two tons of premium-quality fairy lights. This will be lovely – I can chat to others, gain new ideas, and more importantly, see the show from the couples' point of view, so that when I next exhibit, I can improve the wedding fair experience for them.

I did indeed see many wonderful suppliers, excited to be chatting to couples about their big day, offering advice and guidance on their particular products and services and fully embracing the opportunity to meet like-minded people. However, I also experienced a vast number of suppliers who made assumptions about me or other prospective clients, hounded people for attention and spoke only about themselves.

I was offered all manner of on-the-day discounts and reasons for booking with them and not the guy opposite. There was an onslaught of "We can", "We do", "We are" and a distinct lack of "Tell us about you", "Congratulations on your wedding" or "How can we help you?"

I also noticed a very narrow portrayal of what a wedding couple should look like on display. Maybe it was just this particular show – I certainly do not like to make sweeping statements. However, had I been visiting with my partner, we would see no immediate nod to any suppliers who embraced same sex weddings and – on closer inspection – a very limited representation of older couples, interracial brides and grooms or even couples larger than a size 12! I understand that suppliers – especially photographers – want to use beautiful images that showcase their best work. What I don't understand is the idea that beauty still seems restricted to a certain size, skin colour or sexuality.

Yet walking around I saw couples from all walks of life, all evidently very in love and equally deserving of feeling valued and finding suppliers that felt excited to be booked for their special day. I hope that they did indeed find their perfect suppliers and went on to have a wedding that centred on who they are as individuals and as a couple.

If you are reading this book, however, you may yet to have identified how to ensure your wedding truly reflects your uniqueness and how to find suppliers that will help you to do that. If that is the case, you are in the right place.

Who this book is for

Having a wedding that is truly unique to you is not about becoming a "bridezilla" or "groomzilla". It's not about disregarding advice from friends and family or disrespecting the expertise of wedding industry professionals. If you are looking for permission to be rude, hard to deal with and single-minded whilst planning your wedding then this is not the book for you.

This is not a book about how to haggle down prices, have a wedding on a shoestring budget or cut corners. It is designed, however, to ensure you spend money on what is most important and meaningful to you, by setting clear priorities based on your values and beliefs as a couple.

If you are concerned that the true meaning of your wedding day might get lost amongst the onslaught of decisions regarding bouquet colours, bridesmaid choices and venue décor, then this book is designed to help you keep a sense of perspective and keep your values at the core of every decision you make.

You may feel pressured into spending money or booking services that deep down don't sit comfortably with your idea of the perfect day. This book aims to help you listen to your instincts and avoid being steamrollered into other people's idea of the perfect wedding.

I aim to help you identify the important distinction between proudly reflecting your uniqueness and simply being different for the sake of it; how to avoid the pressure of needing to "keep up" with or outdo the weddings of friends and family members and instead focus solely on the key priorities in your relationship.

This book doesn't list every question you should ask each supplier, but instead advises you on how to recognise when a supplier shares your values and feels as passionate as you do about your big day. It guides you through some of the most stressful elements of wedding planning and the big day itself so that regardless of venue and guest numbers, first dance songs and bridal gown choices, your day is a calm and happy celebration of your love and commitment to one another. After all, let's never forget that that in its simplest form, this is what your wedding day is all about.

SUMMARY

- Remember that those who have a tendency to treat you less favourably for your perceived differences are themselves the ones who are struggling to live free of societal pressure to conform in some way.

- Question where your limiting beliefs come from and challenge these in order to do the things you've always wanted to do but have been afraid to try.

- Remember that there are no rules to you being yourself, regardless of your age, faith, sexuality or any physical characteristic you possess.

- Do not confuse prioritising your own sense of self worth with being rude or obnoxious to others who offer support and guidance.

2

Pinpointing Your Priorities

When we think of a wedding day – whether our own or as guests – we often think of the visual elements: the colour schemes, the centrepieces and of course the wedding outfit styles of the newly wedded couple. Of course you will want every last detail to be perfect, and I work alongside incredibly talented florists, ridiculously gifted cake-makers and awe-inspiring venues every day to help make each wedding a magical occasion. If you are newly engaged and cannot wait to start planning the style and theme of your wedding that's fantastic – I'm not here to tell you not to (I'd probably be doing just the same as you are now). It's an exciting time and knowing how long I take to choose what to wear as a wedding guest, I can't begin to imagine how much planning I would put into selecting my own wedding outfit!

However (and you may think it a little odd for a photographer to say this), it is important to remember that a wedding day is not all about the visuals. None of my clients have ordered large framed wall prints of their table plans or cufflinks – instead they select photos that have captured a feeling or emotion from the day. It may be the romance of the first kiss, the tears of a proud father giving his son or daughter away or the happy couple laughing relentlessly at the best man's speech. It reminds me time and again that weddings are about the emotions we feel and the relationships we cherish more than the objects we see.

It can be easy (and perfectly understandable) to quickly get caught up in a whirlwind of bridesmaid dress selections and bouquet choices and lose sight of what is really important to you. Indeed, part of the excitement of being engaged is planning and styling the big day, but sadly, this all too often can also lead to a lot of stress, tension and, for some couples, anxiety.

By being aware of your values – both as individuals and as a couple – planning a wedding can become a lot less stressful and allow you to easily define your priorities and focus solely on what matters to you. This increased self-awareness also enables you to stay true to you and resist pressure from others (whether that be friends, family or suppliers within the wedding industry itself) to plan your wedding according their own ideas of how your perfect wedding day should be.

We will look at how to define your values a little further on in this chapter but first, let's take a step back before we move forward with your wedding plans.

Stop! Go Back a Step!

So, you've had the romantic proposal – maybe under a starlit sky in Paris or perhaps whilst eating a TV dinner in front of The One Show. Immediately, talk turns to venues and dates and fingers reach for the phone to tap into Pinterest and search wedding-related hashtags on social media. However, before your thumb gets a bad case of RSI, step away from the screen and think for a moment, not about your wedding day but your marriage. Remember – both at this point in time and throughout the wedding planning process – that they are not the same thing. Whilst you deserve to have an absolute ball of a day – complete with beautiful outfits and mouth-watering catering all captured by an awesome photographer – you also deserve a long and happy marriage, long after the confetti has biodegraded and your wedding day waistline has expanded.

I have known so many couples who have felt such a sense of anti-climax following their wedding day. Months and often years are spent planning and building-up to it and some individuals have spent their whole lives dreaming of the day they walk down the aisle, only for it to be over in a flash and to be left with a sense of "What now?"

So before you plan the wedding day itself, make some plans for beyond this date too. What would you love to experience or support each other with during your first year of marriage? These can be big ambitions (a new job or promotion) or seemingly small, insignificant plans such as trying new restaurants or having a date night once a week. Whatever your plans or goals – write them down and keep them in sight. The fridge is a good place to pin them up – you visit it countless times a day so cannot help but be reminded of all the things you said you want to experience together.

My partner and I have been together for nearly ten years. When we started dating we lived over 150 miles apart and had to make the most of short weekends together, sandwiched between a 3-hour journey to and from home. We wrote down some of the things we wanted to do in these short bursts of quality time – from places we wanted to visit to friends we wanted to have over for dinner – and stuck them on the fridge door. It didn't take long for us to tick off our "bucket list" and we found ourselves adding to it every month and experiencing so much in such short spaces of time. When I finally packed my bags and moved across the country so we could live together, we figured we now had all the time in the world to do these things. We stopped writing lists and got on with our day to day lives. A few years down the line we realised that whilst we were blissfully happily, our work-life balance had become...well... unbalanced. We had fallen into the work-home-TV routine and realised we had stopped going to new places and meeting new people. We made a conscious effort to once again write down our goals and plans for the year ahead and as a result, discovered a whole new list of adventures we wanted to embark on together. Having these desires written down – just like with business goals and marathon training schedules – really helps you to stick to those plans that are important to you.

When in the midst of wedding planning stress – "debating" supplier choices and frustrated by the seemingly endless list of tasks still to tick off – this list of future goals helps to create a sense of perspective and keep what is really important at the forefront of your mind.

Nope – Still Not Time to Get Planning Yet!

I know! I know! You really want to just get on with finding your perfect suppliers that are going to make your day amazing and provide you both with a million marvellous memories. Before you can find these suppliers, you first need to identify what is and what isn't important to you – and at this point don't think specifically in terms of your wedding day.

What are your shared values and commonly-held beliefs? A strong relationship will of course be based on respecting each others' differences, but there will be some key values you both share that has led you to want to make a lifelong commitment to one another.

Sit down together and brainstorm the values that you share and that underpin your relationship – don't overthink, don't be guided by what you think is the right thing to say. Be honest with yourselves and each other. Spend 10-15 minutes doing this and look at the words you have written down. Next, whittle these values down to three – it may take a bit of time and debate but you will end up with the three most important values you share. To give you an idea here are some examples of what you might want to think about:

Family: is spending time with family important to you? Do you prioritise time with family –whether your own children, parents or distant relatives – over expensive holidays and working extra hours?

Career: are you both ambitious and looking to climb the career ladder? Does this take preference over having children or socialising with friends?

Adventure and new experiences: Do you love trying new restaurants, trips to exciting destinations and get bored by routine?

Socialising: Are nights out still preferable to nights in? Are you always having friends over or out and about making new ones?

Security and stability: Is financial stability important? Are you quite sensible with money and not one to spend what you haven't got? Do you like to know you are building a nest egg for the future and will be comfortable financially in later years?

Peace of mind: One or both of you might be a worrier. Your main aim in life might be to minimise stress and anxiety and to avoid unwanted shocks or surprises at any time. Do you simply want to avoid sleepless nights and bitten fingernails?

There are of course many more values you might come up with: physical health and wellbeing, education and personal development, charity and giving back to others. Don't limit yourselves and try to think outside of the box.

Jot these three shared values down on a piece of paper, keep them on you and refer to these at every stage of the wedding planning process. When you experience conflict or confusion you can return to these – alongside your post-wedding plans – and make sure that your decisions, direction and spending are all in line with what matters most to you. It may not seem immediately clear how identifying these values will help with planning your wedding but I have listed some examples below to get you thinking.

Family – If family is one of the most important things to you and your partner, it is highly likely that you will want them present on your special day. This might influence the venue you choose to book – does it need to be large enough to accommodate second cousins, long lost aunts and your sister's boyfriend's best friend's daughter? Are there older family members who have limited mobility and will therefore need somewhere accessible? If there are a lot of children in the family, you may wish to think about entertainment options for them or a children's menu / portion size. You may want your family involved in the planning process to ensure that they enjoy the day as much as you do. Perhaps asking guests to RSVP along with a song choice for the evening's disco is something to consider. You might meet a fantastic award-winning photographer whose work you love, only to find out during the consultation that you need to spend 2 hours away from your family and friends in order to capture the type of images he/she specialises in. By having identified that family is one of the most important things to you both, you may decide, on reflection, that this isn't the right photographer for your day. It is far better to make this difficult decision now than to regret spending hours posing whilst wishing you were laughing and relaxing with loved ones.

Adventure and new experiences – If you are a couple that loves adventure, trying new things and going to new places, is the traditional wedding going to really feel like you? When talking to wedding suppliers, how excited are they making you feel about your big day? Are they a cake maker who loves new designs and exploring ways to push their creativity? Is that DJ excited by the idea of not having to play the Macarena or YMCA for the thousandth time? Does your photographer like to be pushed a little out of his or her comfort zone? Whereas couples who prioritise stability and/or peace of mind may wish to work alongside experienced suppliers offering traditional services and tried and tested techniques; as an adventurous couple you may be willing to take a risk on hiring that new experimental photographer or book a wedding stationer who creates really "out there" invites and place names. You may even decide that a destination wedding is what you truly desire and so this might be your priority over having every single loved one and family member present.

Career – At first thought, it may be a tenuous link to connect your perfect wedding with your drive and ambition for a successful career. However, your wedding may have to be scheduled for a time when your career demands are not as high, you might prioritise investing in your business or a course of study over that 5 tier cake, or with work taking up such a significant amount of time, it may be worth your while investing in a wedding planner to do a lot of the organising for you. You may be inviting colleagues and need to consider the suitability of the evening entertainment and have to ensure a certain level of decorum is maintained so as not to jeopardise your professional reputation.

These are just a few examples, but hopefully you are starting to see that a wedding that truly reflects who you are is much more than just "I love roses so I want roses in my bouquet" or "We met at a car rally so we are having little fondant cars on our cake". It also starts you thinking about the type of people you identify with and are naturally drawn to, so that when you meet potential suppliers you are not so easily drawn in by sales patter and marketing tricks.

Remember when first defining your values not to think specifically about your wedding. It's all about fitting your wedding around your values and not overlooking your values in order to have somebody else's idea of "The Perfect Wedding".

Another simple exercise you can do – as well as or instead of defining your specific values – is to decide on three things you definitely do want at your wedding and three things you definitely do not. This is a very quick exercise but again – if written down and kept on you – can prevent you from being swayed by pushy suppliers or well-meaning family members. My list would look something like this:

Definitely Want

- *All close family members present*
- *Photography by my favourite wedding photographer*
- *A venue that lends itself to fantastic photography both indoors and outside*

Definitely Do Not Want

- *Cheesy music at the reception*
- *Any tradition that is specific to gender e.g. being "given away" or the groom's speech*
- *Uncomfortable black tie attire*

So now you have a stronger sense of what is important to you and how your values can help set wedding priorities, we can begin to think more specifically about planning the wedding that truly reflects you.

SUMMARY

- Think about your marriage and what that means to you both before thinking about the wedding day itself.

- Make plans and set goals for the first year of marriage and beyond. Write these down and revisit them frequently to maintain a sense of perspective and ensure your wedding day is just one adventure in your lifelong journey together.

- Identify shared values and beliefs that are intrinsic to your relationship. Use these to set priorities for your wedding.

- Remember to fit your wedding around your existing values and priorities and not to lose sight of what is important to you in order to have somebody else's idea of the perfect wedding day.

3

Celebrating Your Uniqueness

To me, feeling or trying to be different from everyone else and celebrating your own uniqueness are two very different concepts. When we talk about feeling different we often at the same time equate that to comparing less favourably to others – possibly in how we look, act, achieve, earn etc. Alternatively, we sometimes go out of our way to be different from others because we compare them less favourably to ourselves. We cannot be or feel different without looking and focusing on the traits and lifestyles of other people.

When we talk about uniqueness we focus solely on ourselves – our own individual skills, abilities and attributes. The term unique has a much more positive connotation and allows us to focus on ourselves as individuals and be proud of who we are, regardless of the appearance and accomplishments of those around us.

We are all unique. Not simply as a result of our age, sexuality, religion, waist measurement or any other singular trait, but by the combination of our individual experiences, values and lifestyles. It therefore goes without saying that the relationship you are in is also unique, with its own set of norms and idiosyncrasies. This is something that I feel passionate about celebrating and reflecting in my photography.

Uniqueness isn't about being something new or changing anything about you, it's about the opposite – not altering in response to pressure or influence from others. So many clients I speak to put off their wedding or photoshoot until they are a certain size or in some way or other feel happier about themselves. We all want to look our best in front of the camera – that is perfectly understandable – but sometimes we equate "looking our best" to "looking as close to how society wants us to look as possible." The idea of a "dream wedding" is very subjective – it will mean something different to every couple and yet we do still see a very narrow depiction of what "perfect" weddings and bride and grooms should look like. Ignore this!

There was a time when weddings always took place before having children, a time when people never married for a second or third time and of course, until very recently, a time when members of the same sex could not marry each other. Why, then, get so caught up in what society thinks a wedding should look like when it constantly moves the goalposts?

Yes, search online for inspiration, have boards for outfit ideas and wedding cake inspiration but let this research help identify what suits and is in tune with you instead of allowing it to influence decisions that may not actually be based on your own inner ideals.

The biggest problem with having a wedding that is "perfectly on trend" is that by the time you look at your photos in a year's time, chances are certain aspects of your wedding will now be outdated! Surely it's best to look back in years to come and remember how fun and perfectly unique your wedding was and to know that if you had gotten married three years previously or three years after your wedding date, you would do it all exactly the same as you have done?

However, it alarms me how – even in our diverse and eclectic society – so many of us feel pressured to have an "off-the-shelf" wedding that ticks all the boxes with regards to tradition and etiquette, even when many of these traditions do not apply to who we are as individuals.

Your Own Unique Wedding Day Vs Being Different for the Sake of It

Don't get me wrong, there is nothing wrong with tradition and if this is something you embrace then you absolutely should plan a wedding that follows time honoured rituals and practices. Whilst I value diversity and individualism, I'm also a huge believer in not being different for the sake of it – especially when it comes to planning your wedding day.

I have heard other wedding suppliers berate couples for choosing "out of date" colour schemes, "predictable" first dance songs and wedding cakes that "look like everyone else's" but if all of these are selected because they truly mean something to the couples in question then no one should make judgements on such choices.

So if you want your first dance to be Ed Sheeran's Thinking Out Loud because it was playing when you met or because it is the song that means most to you both, go for it and don't worry for a second about whether it was one of the most popular first dance songs in 2016 or not. Similarly, if you're not a huge fan of 5-tiered semi-naked cakes, don't choose to have one just because they are in vogue and your friends had one at their wedding.

Trying to be different for the sake of it, attempting to "impress" your guests, or seeking to "outdo" or "outspend" recent weddings you have been a guest at, will not result in a wedding that truly reflects or indeed celebrates you. Don't do yourselves a disservice by deliberately trying to fit in or stand out.

Here are a few more examples of being different for the sake it vs being unique and true to you.

§

Different for the Sake of It
You hate the countryside and don't really fancy a rural wedding but you are the last of your friends to get married and they all had urban-themed weddings so you book a barn wedding to make a point of not copying them. It's cold, your shoes get stuck in mud but hey – they can't say your wedding wasn't different.

Unique and True to You
You know your venue is the same as where your friend got married 2 years ago but you absolutely loved it there and don't care if people

think you're being unoriginal as you can't imagine saying your vows anywhere else. It's a different date, you're a different couple and you know that there are many other factors that will make your day unique – namely the love you have for your partner.

§

Different for the Sake of It

Everyone – and I mean everyone – you know is having Morris the Magician at their wedding. You've loved magic since you were a kid and always planned to book a magician for your special day but it's "old hat" now so you decide against having any magician at all.

Unique and True to You

You've loved magic ever since you were a kid but – despite Morris the Magician being the go-to guy who everyone says you simply must book – you personally prefer another magician who you met at a recent wedding fair. You book your choice of magician and despite one of your opinionated guests telling you that you should have listened to them, he does a fabulous job and provides one of the day's highlights!

§

Different for the Sake of It

The Blitherington-Smyths held a fabulous wedding last summer where money was no object. It was the talk of your social circle for months on end, especially the horse and carriage arrival of the bride and the Michelin starred catering. However, what ever the Blithering-Smyths can do, you can do better. You set a huge budget and spend 2 years and all your savings ensuring your wedding outdoes theirs in every

way. The plans cause lots of tension between you both and you spend
the whole day checking the 'OK Magazine' photographer has captured
it all. You totally forget the reason you married in the first place, the
days and months after the wedding prove to be a huge anti-climax
and you forgot what you ever used to talk about before the engagement.

Unique and True to You

Everyone is still talking about about the Blitherington-Smyth
wedding but not for the right reasons. You have the funds to match
their wedding budget but they are reserved for the renovation of
your first home together and for the trip-of-a-lifetime honeymoon.
You still plan a very stylish and beautiful wedding, but scale it down
a little and remember that the vows are the most important element
and there are lots of exciting plans to put into action following
the big day.

§

The Other Big Question

There will be many people around you who have more experience of
wedding planning than you do. Whether that be friends and family
members who have been recently wed, or suppliers who spend their
working lives making people's special day that extra bit incredible.
Well-meaning words of advice will be offered to you throughout
the planning process (whether asked for or not) and some of this
will be incredibly useful – being independent and focused on your
own idea of what the perfect wedding means to you doesn't mean
you cannot listen and learn from the experiences of others.

However, when making decisions (especially the big ones such
as venue, outfits, guests, photographer etc.) question why you
have made each choice. Have you chosen the local Grade II listed
building because you fell in love with it as soon as you walked

through the doors or have you booked it because – despite it being a little over your budget – your photographer told you it was perfect for creative wedding images and you'd be a fool not to get married there? Are you inviting everyone from the office – including the temp whose name you don't actually remember – because you want everyone you know and love to be part of your big day – or did you feel obliged to because that's what Debbie in Accounts did?

For each decision take a step back and think "Why have we made this choice?" and make sure that the answer is "Because it feels right to us" or "It is important to us and fits with our values". If, on reflection you feel that you are doing something because a friend, family member or supplier made you feel like you "should" be doing it – it might be a sign that your wedding is veering off from being perfectly true to you.

There will be people who genuinely want the best for you and their suggestions and input will come from a place of compassion. These are the people who know and love you for exactly who you are and you will know who these individuals are in your life. There will be others who try to impose their own taste, style and even prejudices upon you and it may at times be hard to stand firm regarding your own decisions, but remember that no-one is more equipped and better informed to plan your own wedding than you. Yes, you may need help from loved ones and require advice from experts but your perfect wedding starts and ends with you embracing and celebrating what makes you unique. Be unapologetically proud of who you are – there will never be another couple like you!

Limits to Total Creative Freedom

You may be forgiven for thinking that so far I have advocated having a wedding free of any constraints or consideration for other people. That definitely is not the case. There are of course a few factors that put a small limit on how wonderfully individual your wedding day can be. Nevertheless, factors such as practicality, legality, budget and health and safety are your only limits – opinions, peer pressure and tradition are not.

Practicalities – There may be certain aspects of your dream wedding that are simply not possible for practical reasons. For example, a ten tier fruit cake is probably not going to be structurally sound, so a compromise may need to be made if that forms part of your ideal wedding day. This is not someone saying that your values or ideas don't matter, it is simply a case of being mindful that what on paper seems a brilliant idea might, in reality, not be in your best interests.

Legality – I'm no legal expert but I do know that there are some legal limits on certain aspects of your wedding day. For example, if you are not marrying in a place of religion you are not allowed to have any musical or verbal content that can be deemed religious in tone or nature. Your venue and registrar will be able to advise you further on this and the reasons behind these limitations. It might be frustrating or annoying to find out that certain plans you had in mind are not possible, but remember the bigger picture – the reason you are marrying in the first place – and don't dwell on things you have no control over.

Budget – Everyone has a budget and even if yours is more Pippa Middleton than Pauline Fowler, sometimes compromises will need to be made. Knowing your values and priorities from the off can help you to prioritise your spending in these instances. However, it is also an opportunity to be wonderfully creative. Throwing money at your wedding doesn't automatically result in style and taste, so don't be a slave to the budget – spend money on what you value and every penny will be worth it. Even if money is no object, try to remember there is a lifetime of adventures ahead that you may wish to spend money on. At the same time, don't be embarrassed or feel the need to apologise for having the money to have the lavish wedding of your dreams. Just don't spend money to impress.

Health and Safety – It of course goes without saying that the health and welfare of you and your guests is paramount. So cramming an extra 50 guests into that vintage barn or on that Thames River Cruise is just never going to happen. Again, this is for your own benefit and not somebody's way of pushing their own agenda or ideals onto your wedding day.

In basic terms, if it's doable, affordable, legal and doesn't endanger or pose a serious threat to you or other people DO IT!!! If you are second guessing yourself because an aunt, a workmate or a supplier turns their nose up at your ideas...DO IT!!

OK So Remind Me – How Do I Be Unique and Plan a Wedding That Is Unique?

You don't need to try be unique – you ARE unique already! By making decisions based on your own likes and values, your wedding will automatically be unique too.

A good exercise is to imagine that weddings are totally private affairs where no guests are allowed and no photos could ever be shown on social media. There is no one to impress and no one to judge you on your choice of outfits, venue and catering. What would that wedding look like? Would any of the decisions you have already made change, knowing that it was not an opportunity to outdo your friends and family or be criticised for your choices?

Start from that place; free of judgement and influence and filled with your ideals and work backwards through the steps, working around any practical, legal and financial restrictions that may need to be taken into account in order to have that wonderful true-to-you wedding. Treat obstacles as challenges and as an excuse to be creative and before you know it – your wedding will be wonderfully you.

Summary

- Focus on your individual qualities and do not waste time comparing yourself to others. Our skills, strengths and achievements are not enhanced or diminished by the characteristics and actions of others.

- When planning your wedding, be guided by personal preferences and tastes regardless of whether those tastes align with current trends or fashions.

- If features of your wedding happen to be vastly different from the weddings of friends and family that's great, but do not go out of your way to be different for the sake of it.

- Learn to recognise the difference between advice and guidance provided in your best interest and people forcing their tastes and ideals onto your wedding.

4

Minimising Wedding-related Stress

Planning a wedding is one of the most exciting tasks that you will undertake together as a couple. It's a chance to celebrate the love you have both found with all those who have supported you on your journey towards this special milestone. You can take this opportunity to be creative and make the day as unique and individual as your relationship. Of course, for many of us, planning a wedding also comes with a certain degree of added stress – regardless of whether you are naturally an anxious person or not. We are not all professional project managers with experience in coordinating the services of a dozen or so suppliers, and liaising with a whole host of professionals you have never worked with before can be a daunting task. So if you are getting a little flustered, cut yourself a little slack; you are not superhuman and there is never more than 24 hours in a day – everything will get done on time and your day will be wonderful...breathe deeply and stay positive.

A little stress (in any area of life) is OK – it can help us to be more productive, meet deadlines and push ourselves to achieve things we did not think ourselves capable of. However, constant worrying, losing sleep, feeling anxious and permanently being in a state of heightened tension is damaging to our health (both physical and mental) as well as to our relationships and overall quality of life. If these feelings are creeping into your life during the months leading up to your wedding, this chapter provides a few simple tools and ideas for reducing your blood pressure and restoring a sense of calm and optimism before your wedding day.

Prevention Is Better Than Cure

Taking the time to carry out some of the activities in the previous chapters and identifying your values and priorities before securing the services of your preferred supplier will play a huge role in minimising stress before your big day. Having identified what is important to you and found wedding experts who not only respect but share your values will allow you to trust in their professional ability to create the wedding day of your dreams.

I do understand how difficult it can be to say "No" to pushy and persuasive sales types, but as hard as it may be to do this at a wedding fair or open evening, think how much more stressful it will be when trying to deal with them a month before your wedding when you realise they do not have your best interests at heart and your day seems to become more and more about them and how they prefer to work. Trust your instincts about people and their services and remember that if it doesn't feel right, they probably aren't the supplier for you.

Identify the Source of the Stress

As I have mentioned, a little bit of stress is common and no cause for alarm. When you do start to feel that these feelings are impacting on other aspects of your day-to-day life, take a little time to sit and question what the specific cause of this stress is. Pressure to meet deadlines and coordinate suppliers is perfectly common and understandable. Pressure to conform, please others or prioritise aspects of your day that aren't meaningful to you, is not something that should be accepted as unavoidable.

Do not underestimate the value of open communication and honesty – right from the start of the planning process – with all people involved in your wedding. Whether you feel pressure or conflict from friends, family members or wedding professionals, be honest about any concerns that you have and politely explain how you might like their approach to alter slightly to be more in line with your ideas. In most cases, these people will be horrified to think that they have caused you any unnecessary stress and be keen to resolve any issues quickly so as to get things back on track with minimal fuss.

For the rare few who still insist on you doing things their way and who continue not to listen to you, stand your ground and explain that they may cease to be involved in your wedding if they do not respect your wishes and individual requests. Some of your plans may need to be restricted for reasons that relate to practical issues (for example your photographer needing to do the group shots at your winter wedding as early as possible before daylight fades) and that is a fair compromise. If conflict or feelings of pressure have arisen for no apparent practical reason, do not be afraid to be firm when explaining how you want your wedding day to unfold. There is no need to be rude or confrontational but there is just as little need to be apologetic for being yourself and having a strong sense of what you want.

Make Lists and Write Things Down

Not a radical idea I know, but one that does have a massive impact not only on productivity but also on feeling good about how much progress you are making. Splitting lists down by months, days or by who is responsible for each action can be a good way to get some of the stress and worry out of your head; essential for a perfect night's sleep.

Making lists doesn't have to be restricted to the things you have yet to do though. Sometimes a page full of unticked items can be depressing and daunting in equal measures so counteract them with more creative lists. You can start by writing a list of all the tasks that you have already completed, which always provides a great mental boost, but how about a list of the top ten things you are looking forward to about married life together, or five reasons why your wedding is going to be wonderfully unique?

If you love lists the world is your oyster; ten favourite songs you're looking forward to dancing together to for the first time as a married couple, the ten guests most likely to drink too much? OK, it sounds silly, but if you are getting really stressed and anxious, this activity does help to remind you that your wedding is a fun occasion and not an arduous exam you have to revise for.

Set Up a Separate Email Account

Web-based email accounts are free and easy to set up. Create one specifically for all correspondence related to your wedding day; provide this email to the relevant suppliers and any friends or family members who are involved in the day. Not only does it save time sorting through your personal account to find emails dating back to the first wedding fair you attended, it also means that you are less likely to miss any important messages from a supplier trying to contact you in amongst Pinterest recommendation emails and Ocado offers.

Most importantly, a separate email account for your wedding enables you to control when you view these messages and means that whilst you may need access to work or personal emails throughout the day, you can restrict how long you spend sorting through supplier messages and organising consultations and be able to set aside specific times to do so. This really helps to prevent your wedding dictating your daily activity and keeps you feeling in control. Do you really want to hear the dreaded ping of an email from a pushy florist just as you are about to relax and watch your favourite boxset?

Keep a Sense of Perspective

You are investing a lot of time and money into having the wedding that you dream of; it's understandable that you want everything to be perfect and for the suppliers that you are paying good money for to provide a service that is exactly as you have requested. As much as every aspect of your wedding is important, try not to overthink every single detail on a daily basis. It is very easy – in all aspects of our lives – to start to obsess over the smallest of things and for these to become bigger and bigger issues than they need to be.

Take a step back, remind yourselves of what is most important to you (hopefully you will have written a list before you started the planning process) and assess whether what you are worried about is going to have a major – if any – impact on these priorities. If your ideal day centres on your guests having fun and the food being perfect, will the shade of chair covers really have an influence on that?

If you start the day engaged and end the day married, you've pretty much nailed this wedding lark and everything else is a huge bonus! Yes, I am being overly simplistic but sometimes it's helpful to think in these terms at 3am when you are wide awake with 5 weeks to go and you can't decide whether to buy the best man Prosecco or Malbec as part of his Thank You gift!

Remember; a wedding is simply the start of your life together, not the end of an 18-month event planning project. As I have already suggested, plan goals and activities beyond the wedding to help keep the wedding an exciting and important day in your life story – but not the be-all and end-all of your relationship. Whether you are planning to have children, go travelling, advance your careers or restore an old property together, don't lose sight of these exciting adventures that lie ahead when stressing over colour schemes and centrepiece arrangements.

Ignore Those "Must-Have" Lists

I love weddings (I wouldn't be doing the job I do and writing this book if I didn't) and I am not for a second belittling the stress and effort that goes into creating the perfect wedding or saying that any aspect of your wedding is not important. I simply do not want you to feel stressed and anxious about elements of your wedding that other people (wedding blogs, publications, family members) have made you feel are important but may not have much meaning to you.

We have all seen these lists online; "10 must have wedding photos", "The must have songs to get your guests on the dancefloor", or "This year's essential wedding theme styles" and hopefully most of us treat these as a bit of fun and take the advice with a pinch of salt. Don't fall into the trap of using these kind of "guides" as the authority on how your wedding should be. It's understandable that having perhaps never been involved in planning a wedding before, your initial reaction when starting to plan your big day is to go online and seek guidance. However, always remember that the day is about you and can be whatever you want it to be. "The Perfect Wedding" (like "The perfect partner" or "The perfect holiday") does not exist – it is a subjective concept. "Your Perfect Wedding Day" does exist – but only by you both being true to yourselves can it become a reality.

There are no "must have" photos, outfits or first dance songs. The only "must" is that each element of your wedding must be reflective of, chosen by and meaningful to you. Do not stress when your ideas of what is perfect doesn't match these so-called experts' ideas. Give your heart and mind a bigger say in your wedding than your social media apps!

Delegate

Being in control of your wedding plans does not mean that you have to do everything yourselves. Whether or not you hand over certain responsibilities to friends and family or wedding professionals, delegating specific tasks and actions to trusted members of your wedding team can help to lessen the stress involved leading up to the big day. Very few of us have the luxury of not needing to work or look after family members, and so by splitting the planning process up into smaller actions and assigning these to relevant others, more can be achieved in a shorter time.

The key to delegation is to try and play to people's strengths – think not only in terms of what tasks people might be best suited to but also what they might be excited and flattered to be involved in. Forcing responsibilities on people who are reluctant to be part of the build-up will lead to a lot more stress in the long term. It is also important to communicate how appreciative you are of their input; not only are you lucky to have a group of people happy to donate their time and energy to help enable you to have your prefect day, you are also much more likely to maintain and inspire their enthusiasm if they feel appreciated and valued. Don't take it for granted that parents, best friends or siblings will have the time to help you, and always be clear about expectations and deadlines that need to be kept, so that everyone knows where they stand and how their role plays a part in the big picture.

You might decide to hire the services of a professional wedding planner to take away some of the stress of planning the wedding. Wedding planners can help you to select and coordinate the best suppliers for you and organise a large majority of the day's events. It is extremely important to find a planner that specialises in bespoke weddings and spends a lot of time listening to your ideas and preferences. Asking potential wedding planners about the range of wedding suppliers they work with can help you decide how bespoke they can make your wedding. The more suppliers a planner knows, the more choice you will have and the higher the likelihood that you will be able to find wedding professionals that share your values. A good wedding planner will not dictate which wedding professionals you should hire and instead provide you with a shortlist of each type of supplier based on your discussed requirements. Be aware that some planners have a set team of suppliers that they recommend to their clients and as a result may not be able to help you to plan a wedding that is truly unique and instead deliver a more off-the-shelf package.

Stay Healthy

Looking your best on your wedding day is not achieved through crash diets, drastic surgery, or excessive exercise you have not sensibly built-up to. However, eating healthily and factoring in time for some regular exercise in the lead up to your big day will help you to feel physically and mentally sharper and feel able to cope with any stresses or unexpected issues that may arise. Sleep is another key ingredient to looking and feeling your best. Nerves may limit your ability to have a perfect night's sleep the day before the wedding, but getting into a good routine in the weeks and months beforehand will really help to keep you energised and feeling positive as you plan the big day.

I'm a firm believer that nobody needs to dramatically change their appearance in order to be wedding-ready or photogenic. However, the healthier you feel both physically and mentally, the less stressed you will feel and the more relaxed you will look in your wedding photos.

Coping with Stress on the Day

Sometimes, we don't always know how we are going to react in unknown situations. Whether your wedding day is your first or your fifth trip down the aisle, a few nerves and feelings of anxiety could surface unexpectedly and this is perfectly normal. If you are of a nervous disposition generally or suffer from any form of anxiety disorder, these nerves may be heightened somewhat. In these instances, there are a few things you can do to minimise and cope with these feelings of tension and stress.

Talk to someone – it goes without saying that you should be honest with each other as a couple regarding how you are feeling before and during the big day. However, there may be times during the wedding day itself when you are not together (possibly during the morning preparations) and so choose a friend or family member who will be with you throughout the course of the day to confide in.

Talking through your worries and explaining what they can do to help keep you calm on the day will instantly make you feel a little less stressed. Be honest about what it is that is making you nervous – perhaps you are worried about being the centre of attention, or concerned the best man will forget the rings. However insignificant or silly you think your worry is, don't feel embarrassed to share your concerns. Bottling it up doesn't help anyone and if people know to expect you to be nervous on the day they won't panic if you are a little quiet or snappy on the morning of the wedding. Maybe having some music playing helps you to feel calm, maybe having the TV on in the background stresses you out even more – share this information with at least one member of your wedding party so they know how to help you on the day.

Plan times for a breather – your wedding day will go quickly, but with a little planning there are several opportunities for you to take bit of a breather and regroup. If your wedding ceremony is at a different location to the reception, the journey between venues is a perfect opportunity to enjoy your first chat and chuckle as a married couple. Don't worry about slow moving traffic or whether you are making good time; enjoy this little lull in proceedings and relax. Another great opportunity to take a break and breathe deeply is during your romantic couple shoot (if you choose to have one). Us photographers have long lenses so we don't always need to be in your face or barking orders – relish the break from talking to guests and enjoy each others' company. I love images where couples are chatting, smiling, kissing and 'taking five' together – they make for such naturally beautiful images. Remember that as it is your day, you can decide how the day's events unfold and whether you will need opportunities to regroup and take a breather. Let your wedding suppliers know this in advance.

Above all, remember to smile; you have met and are marrying your perfect partner. How lucky you are!

Summary

- Recognise that a little stress is good for productivity and perfectly normal but be aware that if it starts to impact your day-to-day life, you may need to identify the cause of the stress. Meeting deadlines and liaising with suppliers is a legitimate reason to get a little flustered; pressure to conform to the ideals of others is not.

- Tell at least one close member of your wedding party if you are feeling anxious (either during the build-up or on the day itself). Not only will the act of opening up immediately make you feel a little better, someone who has "been there before" may have some wonderful words of advice.

- Make list-writing fun. Aside from tedious and lengthy to-do lists, write lists on things you are looking forward to on your wedding day. However, take online "Must Have" lists with a pinch of salt and give your heart and mind a bigger say in your wedding than your social media apps.

- If you know anxiety may rear its ugly head on the big day, factor in some "breather times" throughout the day when you can escape the madness and take some deep breaths.

5

How to Survive a Wedding Fair

At their very best, wedding fairs can be an uplifting, exciting and time-saving experience wherein you meet all of your perfect wedding suppliers in one location and come away with 90% of your wedding sorted in the space of a single afternoon. At their very worst, they can be a depressing cocktail of hard-selling suppliers battling for your attention (and money) and one-syllable wedding supplier wonders, hidden behind their exhibitors' stand, glued to their mobile phones. Most fairs tend to fall somewhere between the two and, whilst you may have to dodge a few gift-of-the-gab salesmen at each event, you will usually find at least one or two ideal suppliers at a wedding fair, providing you have done your research beforehand (more on this later). The main advantage of wedding fairs is, of course, the opportunity to meet suppliers face to face and instantly discover if they are a good match. No website – however wonderfully written and presented – can replicate meeting suppliers in person.

Whilst having an open mind and respecting the expertise and knowledge of the wedding suppliers at each fair is essential, attending your first wedding fair can be overwhelming without first having a basic idea of the style, size and scale of the wedding you are planning.

Some suppliers can be very persuasive, and are skilled in "advising" couples on what products / services they should prioritise (which, coincidently, often involves not only booking themselves but also paying for their most expensive package). It can be easy to be drawn in to these sales techniques, so avoid signing anything on the day and don't be afraid to say that you need to go away and think about it.

When to Attend Your First Wedding Fair

There are no hard and fast rules regarding when you should or should not start attending fairs (although once you are actually engaged would be advisable unless you're looking to drop a very big hint to your yet-to-propose partner)! However, a few factors may influence when you start your grand tour of local wedding fairs.

Before or after you have set your wedding date – there are pros and cons as to whether you start attending fairs before or after you have a date confirmed. Some suppliers will not be able to confirm availability and prices until a date is set. However, if your wedding date is less important than having the perfect suppliers, you may wish set your date according to when preferred suppliers are available (especially venues). This of course all links with your priorities and values and is another reason to look at these before wedding planning starts.

Supplier availability – popular suppliers, especially photographers and venues, often book up 18 months to 2 years ahead. If you are looking to book the "go to" suppliers, make sure you are organised and book ahead.

Themed wedding fairs – if you are planning a particular theme such as "vintage" or "Christmas", look out for specific fairs that feature suppliers that may specialise in this look or style. It goes without saying that these may be seasonal (and are certainly less frequent than "mainstream" wedding fairs) so make sure you find out when they are happening and save the date.

Same-sex wedding fairs are also few and far between (and rarely take place outside of major cities) and so planning ahead is also advisable here.

Finding the Right Wedding Fair for You

Location, location, location – or rather, venue, venue, venue. Whilst many wedding fairs can be organised by third-party companies and not the venue itself, the location of a wedding fair usually provides some indication of the type of suppliers you can expect to see (in terms of budget if nothing else). If you are planning a small wedding on a tight budget, attending a wedding fair at the local Grade ii listed castle (whilst a lovely day out) may be a waste of time in terms of finding suppliers that will suit your big day. Similarly, a vintage wedding fair may not feature suppliers that suit your planned black tie reception theme. There is nothing worse than spending your free time visiting a wedding fair, only to discover that none of the suppliers are appropriate for your wedding. This can be a little deflating (just as it can be for suppliers to discover that they are unable to meet the needs of the couples in attendance). Therefore, don't just go to the nearest fair that is taking place.

Do a little online research – most wedding fair organisers advertise the suppliers that are going to be at their wedding fairs. Have a look on the website and social media pages of wedding fair organisers to get an idea of the wedding vendors you can expect to meet at their advertised fairs. If there are links to the supplier websites, take a little look and make a note of the suppliers that you want to prioritise talking to.

Size isn't everything – choice is essential when finding your perfect suppliers, and the more you meet, the more informed a decision you may be able to make. However, engaging with too many suppliers – whether just at one fair or across a number of different events – can lead to added stress and confusion. If you and/or your partner are someone who is a little anxious about making the right choices and concerned about getting swayed by sales talk, smaller fairs with lower numbers of each type of supplier may be for you. I believe it can be far less stressful to meet two or three suppliers of different services that you definitely want to book, than to meet 4 or 5 potentially perfect (or painfully pushy) suppliers of the same service in one afternoon. For example, if you do not know what you want in a wedding cake, and you go to a huge wedding fair and talk to 4 wedding cake makers, all offering different advice and guidance, you are likely to leave feeling a tad flummoxed (and bloated as there are always samples to enjoy). If you do go to a larger fair, don't feel the pressure to talk to every single supplier. If you have done a bit of research, this will help you to prioritise. You may decide to talk only to reportage photographers, or to florists that charge a minimum amount. Don't be bamboozled by the volume of potential suppliers.

<u>At the Wedding Fair</u>

Etiquette

Whilst wedding fairs are a great opportunity to meet and chat to suppliers, remember that there are many other couples there looking to do the same. Ask some basic questions (more on this later) but don't get bogged down in specifics and details. All you need to identify at a wedding fair is whether a supplier's style, personality and approach is likely to suit your wedding – a one-to-one consultation at a later date is the time to talk details and special requirements.

Arriving 5 minutes before the end of the fair and expecting suppliers to talk for half an hour about your wedding requests is not considered good etiquette. However, if a wedding fair is advertised as taking place from 10am to 4pm, you should expect suppliers to be enthusiastic and interested in finding out about your wedding, regardless of whether you arrive at 10.05am or 3.30pm. You should also expect suppliers to not be packing up their stands whilst you (or any other couple) are still in attendance.

Not every supplier will appeal to your tastes (literally when it comes to wedding cake makers). This is not an opportunity to provide a harsh critique or compare unfavourably to other vendors at the event. Be polite, smile and quietly move on. If there are certain types of supplier that you do not require (due to having already booked one or deciding not to use one at all), don't waste their time by talking to them and then declaring that their services are not needed. A simple "Thank you but we have booked our (whatever the supplier is)" is all you need to say before moving on.

Whilst this may sound patronising, and I am sure you would not dream of behaving in such a rude manner, you would be surprised at the lack of etiquette some potential clients demonstrate. Us wedding suppliers are good at biting our tongue but do not really wish to have the need to during what should be a wonderful occasion to meet lots of lovely couples.

Don't Go Alone

Not only can a second person help you to remember and make sense of all the information that will be directed your way, they can also help you to break away from pushy salesman types. If you decide to split up when at the fair, declaring that you need to go and find your other half is an effective escape strategy from Danny the DJ's personal countdown of Top 40 first dance songs.

If you can't attend with your partner, bring someone with you who not only knows you well, but whose input and opinion you value (and is similar to yours). Be open with them before the fair about any priorities or concerns you have regarding your wedding day. For example, if you are shy and quiet and want a photographer that is a little more low-key, make sure your wedding fair accomplice knows this before they start bonding with the loud and bubbly photographer and recommending that you book them for their great sense of humour.

A second opinion is also really useful when you are unsure about a particular supplier. Maybe you loved the photo booth you tried but thought the owner was a bit sleazy. Having a second opinion on your first impression can be beneficial; especially towards the end of your time at the fair when you may be getting a bit overloaded with information and lose a bit of focus.

Walk Around Once Before Chatting

Don't rush to talk to the first stall-holder you see. Take a walk around and take in the atmosphere, make a mental note of the stands that seem to be generating a buzz and those where suppliers seem to be making a hard sell. Look for stands that are a little more creative or stand out – not necessarily the biggest or most elaborate stands but those that – in some small way or another – highlight the creativity of the supplier. This is also a sign that they love what they do and take pride in their services.

Do check if there is a flow of traffic and try to go with it; otherwise you will get too caught up trying not to bump into people and may miss a potentially perfect supplier.

Answer More Questions Than You Ask

It goes without saying that you will have a range of questions and queries for various suppliers. However, be prepared to answer lots of questions about yourself and your wedding – this is often the sign of a supplier who genuinely wants to learn more about you. There are hundreds of suppliers out there who have a genuine passion for all things wedding related and their excitement and interest should be instantly evident.

Other suppliers will bombard you with information about themselves, their products and their services first, before throwing in the odd token question to feign interest in you. An enthusiastic supplier with your interests at heart will be honest about whether their services are likely to meet your needs. They may know other colleagues who would be more suited to your personality or taste and be happy to recommend them.

Observe Body Language

Be wary of suppliers who are sitting down behind their stand and – even worse – playing on their mobile phones. If they do not have the energy or enthusiasm to stand for the duration of a wedding fair and engage with passing couples, they are unlikely to put the effort into your wedding that you deserve to receive. This is especially true of photographers, event planners and other professionals who will need to be active and engaged throughout the wedding day itself. If you don't want your make-up artist checking Facebook halfway through applying your eye shadow, then don't waste time approaching one who is in a social media daze during a wedding fair!

Bring a Pen and Notepad

After chatting to a supplier or two, make a quick note of anything you want to follow-up on and / or something that you will remember them for. For example, "Ross Willsher Photography – had the photo of the bride with her horse, talked about quirky photos ideas, seemed like an all round wonderful man." (OK maybe not the last bit). You will receive a lot of follow-up emails and messages in the days after the fair and it can be hard to remember who is who after a couple of days so writing a few lines to help you distinguish the personalities behind the brands can be really helpful.

Most importantly, jot down how the supplier made you feel – did you feel valued and listened to, did they make you laugh, did you feel relaxed around them? It is tempting to focus solely on products and pricing but remember, you can't put a price on peace of mind and feeling valued.

Stop for a Break

Non-stop wedding chat can be exhausting. Don't feel you have to move from one supplier to the next without stepping outside for a breather or refreshment break. A little bit of time between suppliers (especially those offering similar services) can help concentration and avoid information-overload.

After the Wedding Fair

Rest and Resist!!

Don't do anything straight away unless you have met one or two suppliers that you gelled with immediately and want to book straight away to avoid disappointment. You might come away buzzing and full of enthusiasm which is fantastic, but avoid rash decisions that you may regret later. Don't feel you have to sort through all the flyers, business, cards, offers and promotions immediately. Pop them somewhere safe to return to later.

Identify Your Definitely, Maybes and Definitely Nots

A couple of days later, get together with your partner and review the information from the fair. Sit with your notes, a laptop or tablet to view websites and the promo material you left the fair weighed down by, and discuss your thoughts. For each supplier, group them according to whether you would like to meet them for a follow-up consultation; three piles or columns – Yes, No, Maybe – is the easiest method.

Remember – the most important feature of a potential wedding supplier is whether they will help you to create a wedding that truly reflects who you are. Refer back to your notes and remind yourself of how they made you feel. Don't be swayed by discounts and offers that are only available for a limited time if you weren't totally sure about the supplier themselves.

As mentioned at the start of this chapter, wedding fairs can vary greatly. Essentially, only you know which will be right for you so do your research, take your time and never feel under pressure to agree to anything on the day.

Summary

- Do some research first. Have an idea of the type of wedding you would like and make sure the wedding fairs you plan to visit will have suppliers that match your style and budget.

- Walk around once before chatting to each supplier. Identify vendors who are creating a natural buzz around their stand and those desperately trying to attract every couple that passes them.

- Observe body language; suppliers should be energetic, engaging and enthusiastic – not sat down glued to their phones (regardless of how early or late you attend).

- Don't go alone and make notes on how suppliers make you feel as much as the look and price of the services that they offer. Do not succumb to pressure to purchase on the day – even if a hefty discount is offered.

6

Finding and Working with
Your Perfect Suppliers

When it comes to wedding suppliers, particularly photographers, you will no doubt be spoilt for choice and find it difficult to choose the perfect vendor for you and your wedding. No single supplier will be perfect for everyone; aside from offering differing styles and packages when it comes to our products and services, we also have our own individual set of values and beliefs and as result we market ourselves to particular clients and sectors of society. From a personal point of view, it is important for me to work with clients who are open-minded, respect and value diversity and who value the time and creativity needed to produce high quality images. As a result, no amount of money would persuade me to accept a client that doesn't share these values; the process would feel unnatural and awkward and communication would be difficult. If I am unable to understand and empathise with my clients, I have difficulty in identifying and portraying the unique beauty of their relationship, meaning the images taken would not be of the standard I like to set for myself.

Therefore, it is important for you to look beyond simply the products / services we provide and look a little deeper at the person or people behind the brand to make sure they align with your own identified values and priorities. As I have mentioned before, an award-winning and highly artistic photographer might not understand your desire to spend as much time as possible with your family on your wedding day, and keep you away from them for several hours to get those gorgeous images. Similarly, you may plan to marry at the stunning local manor house but find the staff not very flexible in accommodating your ideas, and you might start to feel that the venue is having too much influence on other aspects of your wedding such as the catering and timings of the day.

In extreme cases, you could meet florists, wedding planners or bridal boutiques offering stunning products but who simply don't put you at ease. No amount of talent, creativity and success is an acceptable excuse for poor people skills, rudeness and bad customer service. Whilst planning a wedding has certain stresses and moments of anxiety, it is possible to find suppliers that help to take much of this stress away and still deliver their services to an exceptionally high standard. You should never have to choose between quality products and good customer service or be made to feel privileged that you have secured the services of a particular supplier. Yes, some professionals are more in demand than others and book up one or two years in advance, but all suppliers should value and appreciate your custom, assuming you treat them with the respect and professionalism you expect in return.

Finding suppliers whose values align with your own and who you can relate to as individuals, not just professionals, can help you to build a relationship based on trust and honesty. Every supplier should respect your ideas and requests and you in turn should respect their professional opinion and advice. Booking someone simply because a friend hired them for their own wedding, they are the closest to you geographically or they are promoting a special offer, is not going to see you valuing them as experts in their profession and trusting them to do the job you are paying them to do. If a supplier takes the time and patience to really listen to you, understand what makes you tick and goes to great lengths to tailor their services to your wedding, it is only fair that you respect their time and expertise. Don't bombard them with emails and phone calls during unsociable hours, chop and change your mind with regards to your requests or expect daily updates on their activities during peak season.

A Good Ear and a Style That's Clear

A supplier that takes a genuine interest and shows clear enthusiasm for you and your wedding is much more likely to listen to you to understand your requests and concerns regarding the products and services you are looking to invest in. However, it can sometimes be easy to mistake this enthusiasm for a supplier that is simply interested in taking your money. So how do you tell the difference?

Firstly, make sure that each supplier has a consistent theme or style to their products / services. This is a good indication that – whilst they may be flexible in accommodating individual client requests – they also have a strong sense of direction and specialise in a particular niche or skillset. A supplier whose services seem to lack consistency may be less of an expert in their field, have a weaker sense of who their market is and simply be trying to book any or every engaged couple in the region. For example, a florist who offers fresh flowers, silk flowers, modern designs, vintage bouquets and whose work looks as if it has been created by several different florists due to the inconsistency in style, may appear to be able to cater for everyone but in fact might not have the expertise or experience to produce work to a consistently high standard. If a supplier states that they can produce exactly what you are looking for but have very little in the way of evidence to show previous examples, be careful about investing in their services.

Secondly, whilst all suppliers are proud of their achievements and take their chosen profession very seriously, a supplier that values your custom and wants to genuinely help you celebrate your relationship will not simply bombard you with information on their products and achievements but instead explain how their skills will help you to create your ideal wedding. Suppliers who truly respect your individuality and not just see you as a walking wallet, will help you to identify whether they are able to meet your needs and be honest if they feel you are better suited to a different vendor. If you feel pressure to book on the spot (either at a wedding fair or during a consultation), or to upgrade to their top package despite you stating that it is not what you are looking for, don't be afraid to say that you need time to discuss before committing. Personally, I would much rather be booked for my photography and personality than because I offered a discount or additional products for booking on the day. I value my client's custom and want them to value my services, therefore to be viewed as simply the photographer with the best offer at the time is not what I aspire to.

Be Open and Honest

As soon as you talk to potential suppliers be honest about who you are and what you value. This is the quickest way of crossing off those suppliers who do not respect you as individuals.

It goes without saying that throughout the wedding planning process you should be open and proud regarding who you are and what you are looking for. If you are marrying someone of the same sex, a different faith or for the third or fourth time (or even all three), let vendors know when you first chat to them. Whilst a huge majority of professionals are open-minded and welcoming of business from all sectors of society, there are sadly still one or two who are not comfortable or willing to offer their services to certain sub-cultures and minority groups. Honesty is always the best policy and saves a lot of time and hassle further down the line.

However professional and customer-focused a supplier is, it is usually very obvious to spot when someone is disapproving of your choice of partner, lifestyle or individual wedding preferences. Be open about what you are looking for from a wedding supplier – especially if certain aspects of your dream wedding differ from the "norm". Avoid suppliers who inform you that you "must have" particular services or styles – this is a sign of them imposing their own ideals and values on you. This is particularly relevant to suppliers that will be present on the day itself – photographers, wedding planners, venue staff etc. As a general rule, personalities are magnified on a wedding day so a supplier that seems slightly pushy and self-important at a wedding fair or during a consultation may become even more imposing on the day itself.

A huge part of having a happy and relaxed wedding day is feeling comfortable in your own skin. If you don't plan on inviting guests that put you on edge and judge your personal choices, don't employ the services of suppliers who make you feel the same – however fantastic they claim to be. As a photographer, I know from personal experience that people look their best when they are relaxed, having fun and with the ones they love. Trust your instincts when meeting suppliers; are they the type of person you want to liaise with for the next 6 – 18 months and spend 12 hours with on the most important day of your life?

Consultation and Asking Questions

Consultations are the perfect opportunity to meet and talk to potential suppliers in much more detail following a wedding fair or viewing their website and / or social media profiles. During consultations there will be time to talk about your specific wedding and determine if their services are a perfect match for your special day. Often, consultations take place at the office or location of the supplier, but this is not always the case. If you are shy in nature or worry about being talked into making purchases that you might later regret, you may be more suited to a consultation in your own home or on "neutral territory" such as a local café or coffee shop so that you feel more comfortable and in control of proceedings.

There are countless blog posts and publications with advice on the key questions to ask each type of supplier. A simple search online will provide you with interrogation lists for any given wedding vendor. Of course there are burning questions you will want to ask and it is always good to research questions regarding issues that may not have even occurred to you – "what happens if you are ill on the day?" is a classic example. However, don't mindlessly bombard suppliers with every 'must-ask' question you have researched, without first having an idea of what would be the most meaningful answer to you. For example, there is no point asking a photographer how long it takes for your photos to be ready after the wedding, if you don't know what constitutes a reasonable timeframe and haven't thought about how long you are willing to wait. Don't also lead with questions about costs and packages – it shows a lack of respect for the skills and expertise of the supplier and you might actually find that you are prepared to spend more than originally planned on a supplier that you really gel with and feel is a perfect match for your wedding.

The most important thing to note is whether suppliers are happy and willing to listen and respond to your questions and respect the fact that what is obvious to them may not be something you have any previous experience of. If you made notes about your initial feelings when meeting them at a wedding fair, has the consultation helped to solidify these first impressions or made you question their suitability?

Reading Reviews

Reviews and testimonials are a great way of finding out more about suppliers you have shortlisted and the customer experience that they have provided previously. Most suppliers will be courteous, professional and take an interest in you when they want your custom. Reading reviews reveals what these suppliers are like once they have secured you as a customer and received your money.

Rather than simply looking at ratings or stars on their own, do take the time to read the individual testimonials. Note that there will always be the odd review that seems at odds with the majority of the feedback so do not be too quick to judge or discard a supplier based on one bad review out of 20, 30 or 40 great ones.

When reading customer reviews, look out for words or phrases that crop up repeatedly; not just in relation to the services provided but also with regards to the supplier(s) themselves. Often you will gain a sense of the suppliers' values and personality this way. For example, you may read several reviews mentioning how closely a florist listened to client's wishes or discover that a photographer was described as "fun and friendly" in several recent reviews. There is no single phrase that is going to appeal to all couples; it is more about seeing whether the vibe you got when meeting the supplier in person matches other people's first hand experiences.

Remember that no supplier will be perfect for everyone. Whilst pricing and quality of services / products are essential factors when selecting your wedding suppliers, do not undervalue the importance of the person behind the brand and their enthusiasm for helping you have the wedding that is unique to you. Look for vendors that demonstrate consistency and a strong sense of their own values and who are willing to apply their expertise to meet your individual needs. First and foremost, trust your instincts and feelings with regards to how comfortable you feel in their presence and be confident that their enthusiasm is a sign that they value your individuality and satisfaction more than your money.

Summary

- Look for suppliers who have a consistent look and feel to their services and products. There is a big difference between vendors who tailor their services to meet individual clients' needs and those who do not have a clear identity and style.

- Be open and honest about who you are and what you are looking for, especially if your wedding day differs greatly from the "norm".

- Ask questions, but do not simply reel them off from a pre-printed list from the internet; have some idea of what response and answers you are looking for.

- Read reviews and look for common phrases and descriptions couples have used to describe the supplier in question. This provides a good indication of their customer service skills and whether your own first impressions of them are verified.

7

Marrying the One You Love
(Same Sex Weddings)

There are many reasons why I love photographing same sex weddings. Firstly, the absence of pressure to conform to age-old traditions often allows for more creative and personalised approaches to the wedding day. I also love that photographing same sex couples makes it easier to break away from overused and generic wedding poses that you often see time and again in straight wedding images, and allows me to think outside the box a little (which I then apply to all couple shoots, regardless of sexuality). However, more than anything, I love being a photographer in a time when love between two members of the same sex is legally recognised and increasingly accepted as no big deal.

I truly hope that in no time at all, same sex weddings will be known simply as "weddings" and the need to differentiate when talking about a gay wedding will become obsolete. However, I understand that currently there are still some challenges facing gay couples planning a wedding in what is still a very straight-orientated industry.

Regardless of whether you are engaged to someone of the same sex or not, both the challenges and advantages of same sex weddings can apply just as much to any couple who are passionate about having the wedding day that they dream of and not simply adhering to what certain sectors of society expect. Therefore, if you happen to be reading this and are marrying someone of the opposite sex, a lot of what is written here can still help you when planning your unique wedding.

Whilst marriage equality has been a fantastic step forward towards a more inclusive society that embraces diversity and values our freedom to marry whoever we so happen to fall in love with, same sex weddings can often still be seen by some as a novelty event or as not having the gravitas of straight weddings. Indeed, I have had friends ask me when my partner and I are getting married as they would "love to go to a gay wedding". Similarly, I have chatted with suppliers who would "love to get a gay wedding in their portfolio." Gay weddings are – like every wedding – about two individuals in love and making a lifelong commitment to each other. To treat a gay wedding as a bucket list item or a token piece of diversity for your business is – in my opinion – to not see beyond a person's sexuality or respect them as an individual.

Unfortunately, there are still suppliers who prefer not to cater to same sex couples and others who – although probably viewing themselves as inclusive – have difficulty in catering to same sex couples without making assumptions or jumping to conclusions. In fact, this is not limited to same sex couples; all too often suppliers make assumptions about their clients based on their age, appearance or even their choice of other vendors. The moment suppliers start pigeon-holing clients, the less personalised a service they are able to provide.

Avoid Assumption Makers

We are all guilty of making assumptions about people from time to time, but as a wedding supplier I feel it is important to take the time to get to know couples and ask lots of questions rather than to presume that particular aspects of their wedding will be dictated by their sexuality (or religion, age or waistline etc.).

Of course the biggest assumption made is often in regards to one's sexuality – whether due to appearance or personality traits. I never assume at a wedding fair that two women attending together are sisters, best friends or girlfriends, but I have overheard other professionals ask them where their fiancé is and why he isn't at the fair. It is the little assumptions like this that can be quite telling about what these suppliers may be like to work with on your wedding day.

When meeting wedding suppliers, listen carefully to the language that they use. Phrases that begin with "I expect you will be…", "I bet you are having…" or "I photographed a similar couple to you and they had…" are small signs that suppliers are making presumptions based on their preconceived ideas and beliefs. This is particularly true if you hear these phrases when talking to potential suppliers for the first time. I have had all of these phrases said to me in both my personal and professional life, and I know how frustrating it can be to feel that people have jumped to conclusions without taking the time to understand and get to know me first. Yes, some gay couples do want to proudly incorporate the rainbow flag into their wedding theme or have a wedding reception to the sound of camp disco classics, many of us do not. We are not all one and the same and it should not be presumed that we are! I actually viewed a blog recently that was all about gay wedding ideas and it was simply a list of items that incorporated the rainbow theme. It really showed a lack of creativity or effort in understanding same sex weddings.

Also, take note of the language used by suppliers online and in print and have a close look at the images that they have used. Does their marketing constantly only make reference to a bride and groom? For example, many photographer packages include "Bridal prep to first dance" coverage and often, suppliers of light up love letters for the dance floor only have images of "Mr and Mrs" on their website. Whilst these suppliers may indeed be 'gay-friendly' (for want of a better term), it does show that they have not actively considered the needs of same sex couples or demonstrated that they value the custom of gay clients.

I was once told that as a gay man I would get lots of same sex clients because I would be able to 'speak their language'. I politely informed the ignorant individual that we are not an alien race and that simple open-mindedness and an assumption-free consultation process is all that is needed to be a fantastic same sex wedding supplier. It's surprising how many many wedding industry experts still fail in this simple approach. It is my experience of people, products and services often not catering to my sexuality that helps me to understand and meet the needs of gay couples, rather than an innate ability to speak a secret language!

Traditions

What is a wedding without its traditions? Well...still a perfectly beautiful wedding actually.

Due to same sex weddings being a relatively recent development, there is obviously not the long history of tradition that so often shapes (if not dictates) straight weddings. At first this can seem a challenge – to plan a wedding with very few protocols that guide decisions and help sort timings for the day can seem daunting. However, it can actually be hugely liberating to not have to worry about following traditions that may or may not be relevant to you and your partner and you will soon enjoy putting your own unique stamp on proceedings. As long as the ceremony itself is legally binding, your imagination can run wild.

It is good to question each wedding tradition and identify whether you are adhering to it because it is relevant and meaningful to you or simply because it's "always done like that at weddings". More and more couples (both gay and straight) are straying from traditions that are not meaningful to them. I have photographed weddings where the bride made a speech, weddings where there was no first dance, weddings where there were 5 best men and weddings where there wasn't a best man at all. More importantly at each of these weddings, no one batted an eye! Aunt Maud didn't keel over in horror, university friends didn't jeer in disapproval and the registrars didn't refuse to sign the register. So don't stick to tradition to please others, it's your day not theirs and chances are they won't care a jot anyway!

For same sex couples there are three options when it to comes to dealing with wedding traditions that stem from centuries of straight weddings.

1. Stick to the script. If there are particular traditions of a wedding day that you really want to keep, do it! You can still have bridesmaids and best men, have your father give you away and deliver speeches that bore and titillate in equal measure!

2. Put your spin on a time-honoured tradition. You may like the idea of certain traditions but want to make it your own or for obvious reasons need to alter it to suit your same sex wedding. For example, you may wish to walk down the aisle together instead of a with a parent or loved one, or both walk down the aisle but separately one after the other.

3. Ignore the traditions completely. An elopement to Gretna Green with two strangers as witnesses is just as legally binding as a wedding with 10 bridesmaids, 4 best men and a congregation of 500 guests. My point? Your commitment to each other is what makes a wedding – not the traditions. Think outside the box and do it your way if there is no aspect of a traditional wedding that resonates with you.

Dressing to Impress (yourself)

Outfit colours and styles are probably one of the biggest traditions associated with a wedding. Once again, as a same sex couple you can choose to embrace the black and white traditional look or ignore it completely. What you wear is probably the most personal choice you will make with regards to your wedding and only you will know what you will feel comfortable and yourself in. This is the single most important factor when choosing what to wear – do you look and feel yourself in the outfit? I know all too well how couples often struggle to relax and be themselves in photos when they are wearing clothes that don't really suit them. Personally, I don't feel 100% myself in a dinner jacket and bow tie and never see any images of me wearing this as truly reflective of who I am. However, for other guys it's a fantastic look.

Looking online for style inspiration is a great start, but nothing can replicate going into a store and trying on outfits until you find the one that feels just right. Don't be too set in your ideas either – be willing to try on outfits that you may never have considered before and make suggestions based on what you think your partner looks good in. You may be pleasantly surprised. I'm a stickler for blacks, greys and muted tones but my partner loves me in bright colours which I would never have even considered had it not been for his onslaught of compliments!

Have fun experimenting with styles together and deciding how you want to appear on your special day. Having said that, stay true to yourself; wearing something that looks good on you will look far better than simply choosing what is in vogue this season. Lesbian couples can both wear a dress, both wear a suit or have one in one and one in the other – there is no set rule and it goes without saying that you shouldn't feel pressure to dress in a way that either fits or actively avoids any stereotypes.

From a photographer's point of view, I always feel that images of couples are stronger when there is some commonality between the outfits, but rules are there to be broken and if you are happy and relaxed your love will shine through the lens beautifully. This leads me on perfectly to the next topic.

Same sex photographers

One of the problems some straight photographers encounter when photographing gay couples is knowing how to direct and pose them. Most photographers (myself included) were taught using straight couples as models and so when directing shoots, there is a predisposition to instruct couples to stand in gender-specific poses. Photographing same sex couples actually provides more opportunities for photographs as both individuals are not restricted by the traditional male / female configurations.

A photographer who is at ease with photographing same sex couples will make subtle changes to the language they use when posing you. For example, "Now one of you kiss the other on their forehead" rather than "Groom give your bride a kiss on her forehead". Once again, it avoids assumptions – especially with regards to the idea that one of you is the more masculine or feminine in the relationship: a personal irritation of mine! If any supplier – photographer or otherwise – asks you who is the man and who is the woman in your relationship, you have my permission to scream blue murder and run for your sanity!!

However, just because a photographer has not photographed a gay couple before, it does not automatically mean that he or she is not the right photographer for you (especially if you are not looking for many – if any – posed shots). By taking a look at their portfolio you will likely be able to identify whether their approach to photographing couples is varied and personalised to each couple, or whether they use the same generic poses for every shoot. Whilst a consistent look in terms of style and composition is a positive sign of professionalism, placing every couple in the same positions doesn't show much thought for actively trying to reflect the individuality of the couples they are shooting.

Planning a same sex wedding need not be any more complicated or stressful than planning a straight wedding. Yes, you may have a few suppliers who don't really wish to offer their services to you but this is less and less of a problem and you will easily get a sense of who is passionate about working alongside you and who is begrudgingly doing it for the money. Having read this chapter, you now know what to look out for when choosing your preferred suppliers and will spot the warning signs straight away when engaging with someone who isn't demonstrating the respect and genuine interest you deserve to receive.

Summary

- Be wary of suppliers who start sentences with "I expect you will..." or "I bet you are having..." immediately after discovering you are marrying someone of the same sex. This implies that they are making assumptions based on your sexuality.

- Pay close attention to the language and imagery of the promotional materials of potential suppliers. Businesses who particularly welcome and embrace custom from same sex couples will go out of their way to use language that is inclusive.

- Identify which wedding traditions (if any) resonate with you and those which you would prefer not to embrace. Remember, it is entirely up to you how your wedding day unfolds – do not be afraid to think outside of the box and create your own traditions.

- When choosing what to wear, choose outfits that are reflective of you as individuals and as a couple. Do not actively try to conform to or go against stereotypes.

8

What Makes a

Great Wedding Photographer?

Everyone's idea of what makes a photographer great varies hugely. Is it their technical knowledge? The kit they use? How creative their work is? How much experience they have? How they treat their clients? Maybe it's a mix of factors, or maybe it's simply a case of whether or not you love their photos. There is no ultimate tool or technique for finding the greatest photographer in the world (especially as there is no such thing as "The World's Best Photographer"). There are, however, ways in which you can identify the right photographer for you and – more importantly – one that sees and photographs you as individuals.

Identifying the perfect photographer for your wedding will come down to your own preferences and what you value most; the visual qualities of the photograph or the personality of the snapper behind the lens. It's important to note that you can have the best of both worlds – a fantastically talented photographer with the interpersonal skills to boot. To help you find them, I have provided a few tips and hints below.

Technical Capabilities

If you are someone who knows their stuff when it comes to photography and are well versed in shutter speeds and sensor sizes, you will no doubt place great value on the technical capabilities of your photographer, and might be less concerned with how they interact with you in the process of getting awesome shots of your big day. This might be especially true if you are a confident couple who love the camera and have no concerns about needing a photographer with the ability to put you and your guests at ease.

Even if you know nothing about photography, and / or are really passionate about finding a calm and considerate photographer that makes you feel comfortable in front of the camera, it goes without saying that you should make sure that you still book someone with the necessary level of ability and talent to document your wedding day with skill and consistency.

You don't have to be Annie Leibovitz (look her up – she's fabulous), to recognise when a photographer's work is below par. Look carefully at how photographers have used lighting, posing and angles to capture couples – do all these elements work together to make people look their best? Are there harsh shadows across people's faces, photos that are too dark or too bright to show all the details in the images or shots of people where they clearly weren't captured from their best angle? If so – however lovely the photographer seems – think twice about booking them for your wedding.

When viewing a photographer's work, see if they have a consistent style and feel to their images across a range of venues and lighting situations. Are they able to produce beautiful photos on sunny afternoons, cloudy evenings and in dark churches? Be wary of photographers who have some shots in bright bold colours, others in pastel tones, a few in sepia and one or two in black and white. This lack of editing consistency shows that they are still in the process of finding their style, and there may be no guarantee that the images you see in their portfolio are similar to what you are going to get! Whilst every wedding is different and I personally edit each shoot at length to perfectly portray the emotions and feel of the day, I still ensure that my signature style is clearly present and replicates the look of my portfolio examples. Even when turning a photograph from colour to black and white, I have a set process that I use to ensure the tones within my monochrome images are consistent.

Most importantly, when viewing the work of potential wedding photographers, identify whether their portfolio demonstrates a knack for producing stunning images of people of all shapes, sizes, ages and genders. Whilst is it fair to say that most photographers have a target market (whether that be older brides, gay couples, Asian weddings etc.), we all differ in body shape and skin tone and a great photographer will be able to portray people from all walks of life in an equally flattering manner. Whilst using 20-year-old, size 0 models for promotional shoots always makes the talents of a photographer look incredible, it does not demonstrate their ability to work with everyday couples who don't have an innate ability to strike the perfect pose as soon as a camera is switched on. There's a big difference between a fantastic photograph of a "real" person and an average photograph of a model, and I believe that the people used in a photographer's portfolio speak volumes about their values, their respect for diversity and the type of clients they are looking to book.

Never completely overlook technical ability and consistency; have a good look at their work and decide if you can see images of yourselves fitting in perfectly to the collection.

Gadgets, Gizmos and Portraying Personalities

All wedding photographers should be using professional equipment to enable them to capture every moment of your wedding in fantastic quality; regardless of tricky lighting and weather conditions. However, the contents of our kit bags all vary as we have our own vision and methods for photographing all the tears and laughter, joy and passion experienced by you and your guests. Some photographers will use a whole range of artificial lighting equipment; others will use solely natural light. Many will carry two camera bodies on them at all times and switch from lens to lens constantly throughout the day, others will use one camera and a maximum of two lenses.

It's important to note that – providing the images are of the aforementioned technical quality – there is no right or wrong way to photograph a wedding. At a wedding fair or during a consultation, some photographers might be very opinionated as to their techniques being the best way to capture your day. I never claim that my approach is the only approach or that it will suit everyone. Some people will meet me, view my work and decide I'm the man for the job, others may feel my style is not their thing and that's perfectly OK. Convincing prospective clients that how I photograph a wedding is their best and only option would be a waste of everyone's time. I want to be booked for my skill, aligned values and personality and not because I backed you into a corner. It is up to you to make your mind up about who your perfect photographer is.

A photographer with confidence, professionalism and respect for their colleagues will not insist on being your perfect photographer or bad mouth the work of other photographers (or other wedding professionals). Listen to prospective photographers talk about their work; they should be able to confidently explain their approach, state clearly the products and services they provide and (most crucially) ask you lots of questions about you and your big day. If the conversation centres purely on their boasts about technical knowledge, the amount of weddings they have shot, and how many colours their album covers are available in, without pausing to find out about your individual needs, slowly back away now! Regardless of whether or not their work leaves you breathless, if they don't have the decency to listen to you and see you as more than just another subject to shoot then yes, you might end up with stunning images but they won't necessarily reflect who you are as individuals.

I have spent many years honing my skills, and my learning and development didn't stop after studying at college for three years and gaining my qualifications. In my free time I am constantly learning new techniques, experimenting with new lighting styles and trying out different types of equipment. However, my approach is not based purely around gadgets and gizmos. I don't feel the need to use every lens and lighting setup at my disposal at every wedding I do. My knowledge and kit give me a variety of shooting options but my passion is for people not products. If I have an extra 15 minutes during a wedding or photoshoot, I much prefer to spend it making sure couples are feeling relaxed and comfortable in their own skin than to add an extra 3, 4 or 5 lights to an already well-lit environment. The most stunningly lit, wonderfully creative, and perfectly edited image means nothing if it doesn't capture you at your best and make you feel good about who you are. If a photographer isn't capturing your personality with one light, they aren't going to change that by adding in extra lighting or changing their lens. Never underestimate the importance of the client-photographer dynamic. Cameras, flashes and memory cards alone are not what brings out your true personality. That can only be done through building a trusting relationship with the person behind the camera.

Visibility and Volume

Another factor to consider when identifying the best photographer for your wedding is determining how visible you want them to be during the day. It goes without saying that reportage photographers do tend to blend into the background a little more and some are barely even noticed, whilst other photographers take much more control and have a greater say on the proceedings and timings throughout the occasion. Once again, there is no single approach that is better than the other. As a couple, have a discussion about what approach you would prefer.

The thought of a domineering, bossy photographer may be your worst nightmare but if you know that you and your guests are going to be a handful and hard to organise (especially when rounding them up for group photos), you may opt for someone with a strong personality and commanding presence. However, don't confuse authority with ego and arrogance. It is possible for a photographer to be assertive and take control at necessary times, without making the day all about them. If you have already booked other suppliers mention to them some of the photographers you are considering booking, and find out if they know what they are like to work with. Whilst they might not have heard of every photographer in the region, chances are they will recognise any names that have demonstrated diva-like behaviour!

It may be important to you to have a photographer who is capable of communicating with every one of your guests and dealing with all generations of your family; from the tantrum-throwing two-year-old niece to the hard-of-hearing great aunt. Being able to interact with a diverse range of people is an essential skill as a wedding photographer in my opinion, but sadly there are some professionals out there who lack the ability to relate to people of all ages and backgrounds. If you have guests with particular needs – whether this be mobility problems, anxiety-related issues, or hearing problems – mention this to prospective photographers and make a note of how they react. Of course, no photographer will say that this will cause a problem or be an inconvenience, but a considerate photographer will ask questions in a sensitive manner and find out how best they can minimise stress and accommodate these needs. When reminiscing about your wedding day, you do not want guests moaning about 'that bossy photographer'.

Assertive and Inclusive – Not Mutually Exclusive

A good photographer should have a clear idea of the shots he or she is planning to take throughout the day and be able to advise you on what to expect when working with them. They should be able to answer your questions with confidence and provide you with peace of mind that you are in safe hands. Despite this, there should be opportunity for ideas and input from you. Obviously they are the expert in photography, but they will need to get to know and understand you to be able to photograph you in a manner that truly reflects who you are. When I offer most couples the opportunity to suggest any ideas they have seen and would like to try, they tend to leave it to me to take total control. Regardless of this, I always give clients the opportunity to feel included and part of the creative process. For me, the art of photography is a collaboration and something all parties should feel empowered to contribute to.

You may decide that you want the photographer to take total control as you have no clue what to do in front of the camera. That is absolutely fine, but however small a role you play in terms of creative input, make sure the photographer is asking you lots of questions and you feel they are genuinely interested in learning more about you.

Venue Experience

One of the most commonly asked questions is "We are getting married at [venue name], have you shot here before?". Whilst experience at a venue can be beneficial, it is far from essential. Photographing a venue for the first time allows me to see things with fresh eyes and come up with creative ways to work within the grounds and buildings. Many photographers who have shot in the same venue countless times can have a tendency to get stuck in a routine of shooting the same poses in the same locations and not provide a truly individual approach to your wedding photography. I always love to visit new venues with my couples beforehand to plan where we can take some stunning images and come up with lots of exciting shot ideas.

It's also worth noting that should you happen to go on holiday with a professional photographer, the chances are, their holiday photos would be a lot better than yours. This isn't because they have been there before, it is because they have the skills, training and expertise to photograph new or unfamiliar surroundings to an extremely high standard. Do not let lack of venue experience put you off booking a photographer that in all other ways seems perfect for you.

And Finally...

As previously mentioned, don't ignore your gut feelings. We are often drawn to people whose personalities and traits seem similar to ours. Whenever I have worked as a "Second Shooter" for other photographers, I realise how their clients differ from the couples who book me and how 9/10 times, my clients are couples who I would choose to socialise and spend time with. It is surprisingly easy to identify when someone seems the perfect fit. Therefore, providing the photographer you naturally feel most drawn to has a strong and consistent portfolio and doesn't come across as a self-obsessed technical geek, pay that deposit and secure them for your big day!

SUMMARY

- Understand there is no single way to shoot a wedding, and avoid a photographer who says that their way is the only way. It's a sure sign that they have little respect for fellow photographers and probably possess an inflated sense of self-importance.

- When viewing a photographer's portfolio, observe whether they have used lighting, posing and composition together to make people look their best. Are they able to produce beautiful photos in a variety of environments?

- Ask yourself whether you can identify with the couples in a photographer's portfolio. Are they all a certain age, body shape or skin colour? Even if a photographer is targeted towards a particular market, they should be able to make people of all demographics look their best.

- Don't be put off if an otherwise perfect photographer has not shot at your venue before. A great photographer is able to capture awesome shots of unfamiliar locations. Often a fresh pair of eyes can lead to fantastically original images.

9

Finding Your Photography Style

Sometimes, when something is such a big part of your day-to-day life, you can easily forget how alien and abstract it is to someone else. It goes without saying that photography is something that is ingrained in me now and barely an hour – let alone a day – goes by when I'm not thinking of or looking at my own work or the photography of one of my favourite shooters. However, a conversation I had with a lovely couple during my first wedding fair reminded me that for many, photography is not an area of expertise.

Having discussed how the couple had met, heard all about the romantic proposal and chatted about plans for their wedding (I absolutely love getting to know couples – definitely a highlight of the job), I casually enquired as to what style of wedding photography they preferred. I was a little taken aback when – after a brief pause – they declared "Umm we're not sure – non-blurry photos mainly!" Luckily I specialise in non-blurry photos so I definitely felt I could live up to expectations there, but it really brought home how as experts in our field, wedding suppliers have a huge responsibility to educate and inform clients regarding what services and styles are not only available but will most suit their needs. Personally, I think there is a huge difference between proudly describing and showcasing your talents and trying to mislead all couples that your product or service is the only viable option for them.

My style and approach to shooting a wedding will not suit everyone, and I feel strongly about being honest with clients as to whether we will be a good fit. A flexible, open-minded approach when listening to clients' needs is hugely integral to what I do, as well as ensuring that everyone feels relaxed and good about themselves both during and after the shoot. However, I do not stray from my own photographic style whilst doing so; the way in which I frame and compose my photographs is personal to me and if clients ask me to recreate a look that is not consistent with my style, it is usually a sign that they are better suited to working with another photographer.

How Much Do You Value Photography?

By value, I don't simply mean how much can you afford to pay a photographer. How important is it to you to have your wedding captured on camera? You may simply want a few snaps to document the day and know that you won't want to adorn your living room wall with a photo of your first kiss or keep an album on the coffee table to ~~bore~~ entertain your dinner guests with at every opportunity. Therefore, it might be that you want a no-nonsense, straightforward photographer who doesn't cost the earth to come and take a few essential snaps and that's enough for you. There is absolutely nothing wrong with that at all (although granted, I'm likely not the photographer for you).

Is having your day captured in a creative and artistic manner more important to you than simply having "nice" photographs taken? Can you visualise works of art from your wedding day forming the backdrop of your marital home for years to come? Perhaps – although you want lovely photographs taken – it is just as important to find a photographer that makes you feel comfortable and who will get on with your guests. Maybe you know of an incredible photographer whose work you have loved for years and are prepared to put up with any diva-demands and bossiness because the images will be 100% worth it.

It might be hard to answer these questions at first, and it may take a bit of research – online and at wedding fairs – to decide what your photographic priorities are. These priorities may also change a little once you have spoken to a few of us photographic whizz kids (holding a sample wedding album in your hands tends to dramatically increase your appreciation and demand for the work we do)!

However, it is far better to know in your own mind what is important to you photography-wise before you meet that pushy photographer who informs you that you need their top package that includes the biggest wedding album in the world, 17 photographers on the day and a magazine spread for the cost of a small mortgage. You then realise a year down the line that the photos haven't seen anything other than the inside of the old chest of drawers in your mother-in-law's spare room, since you returned from your honeymoon.

Paying top dollar for the best of the best is fantastic, but only if that decision has been made by you not the photographer.

Finding a Style That Suits

Line five photographers up in front of you and your fiancé, strike a pose, invite them to snap away and then send them home to edit your images.[1] You would receive 5 completely different sets of images (probably after very different lengths of time but that's another chapter entirely) all shot from different angles at different focal lengths – some would feature just your head and shoulders, others would incorporate all of your surroundings. Some will be bright and light in tone, others would be darker and moodier in their feel. Some may have the look of old-fashioned film cameras; others may have a distinctively modern feel about them. A selection of images would be presented in black and white, others would be filled with highly saturated colours.

My point is this: not one of us photographers view and photograph the same subjects in the same way and this is reflected in both how we shoot and how we edit our work. Yes, there are

---

1   This is a hypothetical exercise – I will not be reimbursing anyone who empties their bank account trying this theory out!

photographers whose style is similar, but when it comes to choice, you will have a far more varied selection of wedding photographers to choose from than any other wedding supplier category.

Have a good look online at photographers, not just locally but across the globe and get a feel of what really resonates with you. However, be realistic; if your research has you swooning over the work of a Californian photographer of beach weddings and you are having a winter wedding in a village church in the Cotswolds, the chances are, no photographer will be able to recreate that look perfectly. I love shooting backlit images by placing couples in front of the sun and creating a soft rim of light around them. However, with Britain not being known for its year-round sunshine, I make a point of not only having just these type of images on my website as it is not possible to replicate them on every occasion.

Some of you will easily distinguish between a photographer who takes "good" photos and those who use light and composition to evoke mood and feeling in their work. Whilst price doesn't always determine quality, I would suggest that if you are struggling to understand why one photographer charges £500 and another charges £5000, you would not be spending your money wisely if you went for the more expensive option. Just as important is not to book the most expensive photographer on reputation alone if – in reality – you don't really like their work. Once again, this is about having a wedding that is true to you and not about showing off to guests about being able to afford the suppliers at the top end of the market, despite not having a true appreciation for their skills.

Photographic styles – like all forms of art and creativity – go in and out of fashion to a certain extent. Be careful about taking guidance from social media; what you like now because it is all over your Instagram feed may not look so good above your dining room table 5 years later. As I have already mentioned with regards to other aspects of your wedding: ask yourself whether this would be your photography style of choice in three years' time or three years prior to your wedding date. Photographs of you looking your best, looking happy, and sharing a wonderful occasion are timeless – faddy editing styles and filters don't tend to be. Remember when everyone had those black and white photos with selective items in colour? Me too – and I cringe at the thought!

Reportage Photography and "Natural" Photos – Not Always the Same Thing

One of the phrases I hear a lot from prospective clients is "We really like your natural photos" which – truth be told – is music to my ears. However, whilst much of my wedding coverage is of a reportage nature (i.e. quietly observing and capturing non-staged moments throughout the day), sometimes even the most natural-looking images have involved a little bit of input and setting up from me. For example, no bride (or groom for that matter) wants to be photographed before their hair has been styled to perfection and so we take a shot of the hairdresser skilfully working their magic after the actual styling has taken place. Similarly, whilst the love and laughter of the newly married couple may need no prompting whatsoever, they may need to be placed in a location where the light really helps to emphasise and compliment these natural expressions and interactions. We therefore relocate to a different part of the venue where they can continue to walk, talk, embrace and laugh in any way that feels natural to them. This is probably my favourite technique when capturing romantic photographs; finding the perfect spot where the light falls beautifully, offering advice on subtle posing or positions and then capturing the moments in between the "proper" photographs – the laughter, the lingering looks of love, the impromptu kisses. Yes, they look natural – they capture you both as you are – but they didn't just magically happen either.

Other photographers shoot exclusively in a reportage nature with no setup or staging whatsoever. There are some incredible reportage photographers out there who will take phenomenal images of your special day without you ever having to stop and pose for a single second. This sort of coverage is perfect if you really want to get on with enjoying your day with your guests and not have to worry at all about group shots, posing or staying away from the bar until you have nailed those creative shots!

However, be aware that some reportage photographers can not always guarantee capturing certain moments if they occur without prior warning regarding when they are due to take place, whilst certain guests may be adept at avoiding the camera and thus not appear in any of your wedding images. If there are certain people you want to remember being at your wedding – such as Great Uncle Ian who has travelled all the way from Scotland in his finest kilt – then adding a few group photos into the mix is a good idea. These don't have to be overly-staged, long-winded and boring but they do ensure VIPs are captured; look for photographers who take a much more creative approach to the group shots for the perfect compromise.

Whilst camera-shy couples tend to prefer reportage photography on their big day for obvious reasons, I often find that this approach works best when both the couple and their guests are naturally animated or expressive. Fun-filled photographs of your family cutting shapes on the dancefloor make for better captured moments than 50 wallflowers looking down at their shuffling feet. There is absolutely nothing wrong with being quiet and reserved – I love working with nervous couples and helping them to enjoy having their personalities celebrated on camera – but a room full of very quiet lethargic guests doesn't provide a great deal of photographic opportunities. Therefore, think about what kind of wedding you are planning in terms of the vibe and energy of the day and how you want this reflected in your wedding photographs. Wedding photographers can shoot from a range of angles and focal lengths and use an array of editing styles, but we cannot photograph hysterical laughter and comical expressions if these are not in existence on the day.

Another factor to consider with reportage photography is how comfortable you are within your own skin. Reportage coverage often captures beautifully natural expressions, gestures and interactions; catching a fleeting moment and transforming it into a keepsake of a lifelong memory. However, it doesn't necessarily hide double chins, flatter curvy figures or eliminate crows' feet. Are you happy to be photographed exactly as the camera captures you or would you prefer photos where you can take a little guidance from a photographer who will gently pose you to enhance your beauty and minimise any self-identified flaws (whether actually in existence or simply in your own mind)?

Choosing your photographer is an important and difficult task, so do take some time to first identify how important wedding photography is to you and secondly gain a brief idea of the style and coverage that will best suit you and your wedding.

If, after consideration, you do feel that you want the whole day captured creatively by an attentive and friendly photographer, don't underestimate their value. Getting to know you as a couple and understanding what makes you unique, spending 12 hours-plus on their feet on your wedding day and committing countless more hours editing and designing your timeless keepsakes requires a vast amount of skill, professionalism and commitment. That's not to mention their time spent continually studying and developing their skills. If you have found a photographer that meets all of your requirements and will create works of art, be prepared to pay them accordingly regardless of their style.

Summary

- Identify how important wedding photography is to you and whether it is a just necessary expense or central to the life-long memories of your special day.

- Spend time online and at wedding fairs looking at a range of wedding photos and identify which sort of images resonate most with you. Is there a commonality amongst the wedding photos you most love? Do they depict romance and laughter? Are they abstract and creative in nature? Is it about the tone and style or the content?

- Think about the vibe and energy of the wedding you are planning and how you want this reflected in the photos. Your ideal day might lend itself to a particular look or approach.

- Be aware that "natural" looking photos often require a little setting up beforehand to get the best light and setting for the shot. Understand that full reportage coverage of your wedding is possible but is not ideal for those who prefer to be posed and positioned in a way that eliminates perceived flaws.

10

Your Engagement Shoot

For bride and grooms-to-be who aren't huge fans of having their photo taken, a pre-wedding / engagement shoot can be something that fills them with absolute dread and horror. The idea of voluntarily having an extra photo shoot on top of a full day of wedding photography, seems like adding to the stress and anxiety that wedding planning can sometimes bring.

However, pre-wedding shoots are in fact perfect for camera-shy couples, nervous bride and grooms and of course ideal for those couples that want extra time starring in front of the camera! They really are a win-win experience!

Some photographers schedule the engagement shoot at the wedding venue itself whilst others prefer a separate location entirely. There is no right or wrong location – do what feels best for you. Wherever your shoot takes place, there are at least 5 good reasons why engagement shoots are a great idea.

It Provides Time to Get to Know Your Photographer

Wait! Forget about all things photography for a second (yes I can't believe I just said that either)! One of the biggest benefits of having a pre-wedding shoot is the quality time you have with your wedding photographer. Getting to know each other a little better during a relaxed shoot means that come the wedding day, your photographer will be a familiar face and not simply a stranger with a camera. Feel free to ask them questions, find common interests and have a bit of a laugh and joke together. If you are nervous say so; you have hopefully booked a photographer that you feel comfortable with and who you can easily talk to, so never be afraid to be open and honest at all times.

You Get a Chance to Practise

I'm not one for elaborate posing that only contortionists can achieve, but simple guidance on the placing of limbs, chins and torsos can really help you to love yourselves in photos. The pre-wedding shoot allows you to practice which stances feel comfortable and flatter you. You can also try different poses over and over without worrying about entertaining guests or rehearsing your speech for one last time. Come the big day, this will make you feel a lot more confident and in control, resulting in wedding photos that will turn your guests green with envy! Remember, natural looking photos always involve a little bit of staging so if your photographer does advise you how to stand and hold each each other, it doesn't mean that you aren't fantastically photogenic, it simply means they are doing their job in helping you to look your absolute best.

Your Photographer Learns More About You as a Couple

I love how every couple I shoot is unique. Meeting different people is one of the highlights of my job and I think it is important that your relationship is reflected perfectly in your wedding photos. A pre-wedding shoot enables photographers to establish the type of couple you are and how best to document this. For example, romantic couples who love to hold hands and cuddle will feel comfortable doing this in photos. However, if you are not a "touchy-feely" couple, it is best to find this out before the wedding day, so we can ensure that how we photograph you isn't at odds with how you see yourselves. You may even prefer some quirky and humorous shots and we can also explore this during the pre-shoot. The more interactive and open you are during the shoot, the better your photographer will get to know your dynamic and can direct the session accordingly. During the shoot do not feel afraid to say "this really doesn't feel like us" because – whilst visually the image may look fantastic – as photographers, we don't know straight away how you see yourselves both as individuals and as a couple.

You Can Provide Feedback on the Images from the Shoot

I find it really useful to chat briefly to couples following the pre-wedding shoot to find out which images they did and didn't like. It might be that they preferred the full length shots as opposed to the close-ups, or that their favourite images were the ones in which they weren't looking directly at the camera. Knowing this, I can ensure that these are the type of shots we focus on during your wedding day, which saves time on the day and allows you to get back to your guests that little bit sooner (if you want to)! Primarily, I see engagement shoots as a practice session for both of us before the big day, so your feedback following the shoot is just as valuable as your input during the session itself.

If, following your engagement shoot, the images are not quite what you had hoped for, don't stress, panic or immediately book another photographer. Take a little time to reflect on what you weren't happy with – was it the posing, the setting, the editing? Contact your photographer and have an open and honest chat – explain your concerns and discuss what didn't work for you. It might be that perhaps communication on the day wasn't as effective as it could have been. Remember, an engagement session is all about making sure everyone is on the same page before the wedding day. It's a great opportunity to ensure all parties are happy going forward. Before the wedding day arrives you will spend time practising and amending your speech, trying on your outfit and rehearsing your vows. Your engagement shoot is the dress rehearsal for the photographs so do not underestimate how much of an important part of the wedding preparation process the session is.

We Can Talk About How Your Plans Are Going and Any Concerns You Have

I advise couples to have their engagement shoot about three months before the big day. This is close enough that any tips or ideas we discuss are still at the forefront of our minds at the wedding, but far enough in advance that it isn't a last-minute stress. It is great to share how your wedding plans are going and any concerns you have – both specific to photography and in general. Wedding photographers know a range of other wedding industry professionals who may be able to assist with any last-minute issues or concerns that you may be experiencing. A pre-wedding shoot is a perfect opportunity to iron out any problems or hiccups. Photographers are one of the few suppliers that will be with you before, during and after the wedding day itself so I personally feel part of our responsibility is to be a guide and source of advice throughout your wedding journey as much as possible.

Hopefully, those of you who were dreading your pre-wedding shoot or didn't quite see the reasons for having one, feel more reassured. It really is nothing to worry about. However, a successful photo shoot doesn't depend solely on the photographer and there are certain things all couples can do to ensure that their pre-wedding shoots are a resounding success.

Remember That the Pressure Is Off!

There is absolutely no pressure or expectation from me for you to magically transform into an experienced model and strike hundreds of dynamic poses as soon I take the lens cap off. Therefore, please do not put pressure on yourself to get everything right first time during the shoot either. This shoot is designed to be relaxed and informal and there is no need to worry about anything on the day. I think patience and empathy are essential skills for wedding and portrait photographers as no matter how many shoots we have done in the past, we must always remember that for most couples this will be the first time in front of a professional photographer. Expect to make mistakes, ask your photographer to repeat things, take a long deep breath and relax – any pressure should be on your photographer not on you.

Ask Questions

My favourite phrases that I love to hear during a pre-wedding shoot are "I don't quite understand that" "Can you repeat that?" and "Am I doing this right?"

Hearing these questions mean that you feel comfortable enough be honest and open which is awesome. You can ask me to explain or demonstrate something time and time again and I absolutely do not mind – make sure you find a photographer with the same attitude.

Also, treat the shoot as an opportunity to ask any questions relating to photography on your big day. Sometimes it is not until you are in front of the camera that questions or concerns will crop up and so vocalise these queries as they arise.

Wear Similar Styles

Most photographers have absolutely no problem with you wearing whatever you want to on your shoot. However, I do advise my couples not to wear all black (makes for dull images) or items that are new or uncomfortable – irritating labels, ill-fitting trousers, or heels normally reserved for Royal Ascot will all detract from you relaxing and feeling filled with romance!

What I do suggest is that you and your loved one dress in a way that complements each other. You may have individual styles which is fantastic, and I'm all for promoting individuality (as you may have guessed by now). However, if one of you dresses for the opera and the other dresses for the allotment, it may look a little odd, but – if this what makes you the couple you are – I'm all for breaking this rule!

Bring Ideas

Your input should be as important to your photographer as my clients' input is to me – from the setting and scene of the pre-shoot to the poses and shots taken, my clients have as much say as I do. If there is a hobby or activity that you both enjoy together then ask your photographer if they can incorporate this – that might be walking the dog, cycling or being down at the stables. You might even want a shoot based around chilling at home. I'm open to all ideas as long as they are practical and hopefully your photographer will be too. I will of course take a lead during the session and will offer a professional opinion about what will work, but please do not feel that your photographer is "in charge" – we are here to work alongside you. You may have seen an awesome photograph that you would like to recreate and if it is possible and practical then there should be no reason why your photographer doesn't value this input.

Saying that, you are more than welcome to leave the ideas to the photographer – again there is no pressure for you to be part of the creative process if you do not wish to be.

Be Willing to Try New Things

As I have said before, photographers are not here to make you look or feel silly in your photos. However, please do trust them when they ask you try different poses. Sometimes to look good in photos we might have to stand or pose in a way that feels at odds with how we would naturally position ourselves in "real life". A good photographer's aim is for you to have fun whilst having beautiful photographs taken. Be open-minded, and trust that everything that is advised and suggested to you is to help you to look and feel amazing.

If you only remember one piece of advice from this chapter, make sure that when you arrive for your engagement shoot you are 100% yourselves! Don't fear the camera, or change to fit an idea of "how couples should look in photos" - be proud of everything that makes you who you are, enjoy each others' company and trust that, in doing so, there is no way that your uniqueness and beauty won't shine through!

Summary

- If you are not comfortable having your photograph taken, an engagement shoot is the perfect opportunity to feel more comfortable with the process and get to know your photographer.

- Use the occasion to ask your photographer questions about your wedding, both in relation to the photography and with regards to other aspects of the day. Photographers are one of the few suppliers who spend time with you before, during and after the big day so can help advise on the entire process.

- Be open to trying new ideas and bring along your creativity too. Have fun collaborating with and building trust between yourself and the photographer.

- Remember that the pressure is off and you are not expected to get things right first time. Ask lots of questions and ask your photographer to repeat things if you are unsure what to do at any point.

11

Simple Tips for Better Wedding Photos

I believe strongly in collaborating and working closely with couples to create the best wedding photos possible. Wedding photos are your lifelong memories and therefore it seems a no-brainer to me that you are actively involved in the process of capturing such treasured moments. Whilst us photographers are experts on the technical aspects of photography such as lighting, composition and posing, the amount of input you have before and during the day can make a massive difference to both the quality and quantity of photos your wedding photographer produces for you.

This chapter looks at just some of the things you can do to help ensure the best possible photographs are taken. It is not an exhaustive list (that's a whole book in itself) and I do not claim to have come up with all of these tips myself. Some have been passed on to me when working with fellow photographers, others have been discovered on blogs and online forums. However, knowledge is meaningless if not shared with those who can benefit most from it, and the more couples that are informed about how to help their photographer take stunning photos the better in my opinion.

Before the Wedding Day

Communicate any anxieties – make your photographer aware of any concerns that you have (especially in terms of confidence or feelings of anxiety with regards to photography). Don't wait for your photographer to turn up to your wedding day preparations before you declare "I hate having my photo taken". Use your engagement shoot to relay these fears, and if you haven't booked a pre-wedding shoot, make sure you meet with your photographer to discuss why you do not feel comfortable in front of the lens and allow them to reassure you and plan an approach that minimises your stress and worries.

Try on your outfits and practise moving about in them – trying on on your outfits before the big day seems obvious, but it is surprising the number of bride and grooms who don't try everything on until the morning of their wedding, only to realise the fit isn't perfect and they aren't fully comfortable. It's hard to enjoy a day when you don't feel comfortable in what you are wearing and wedding clothes can take a little longer to get used to compared to everyday wear. Have a little practice so that walking, dancing and rocking your wedding photos all feel a little easier on the day.

Gather any information requested by your photographer – if your photographer has asked you to find certain things out prior to the big day (and even if they haven't) make sure you have done the necessary research and pass on any important information. Timings are the most important thing to make sure you and your photographer are both up-to-speed on. Knowing when everything is happening and how the photography coverage fits in with the timeline of the day is perhaps the most crucial part of the planning process. Everything on a wedding day takes longer than normal – from getting dressed to eating a three course meal – so timings are always set with a little flexibility in mind. However, your photographer will need to know if speeches are before or after the wedding breakfast (or if they are happening at all), the time of the first dance and other key moments. This is especially essential if you have opted to stray from the traditional wedding format and the flow of the day is vastly different to most weddings.

You may also need to talk to the venue, vicars, registrars and other wedding suppliers about any other rules or restrictions on photography during the day and inform the photographer in advance whenever possible to do so.

Plan your group shots (and any other essential images) – whether you sit with your photographer to produce a shot list or simply jot down this list as a couple, make sure you have written down all of the various group shot combinations you want photographed on the day and your photographer has a copy. I recommend between 6-10 group combinations to avoid the process becoming too time-consuming and boring for all involved. However, this is a rough guide only and very much depends on the size of the wedding party and whether these images are to form a key part of your wedding day memories. Also make sure to share any key shots that you want your photographer to capture – is your watch a family heirloom? Is there a private joke regarding your choice of aftershave? Make sure your photographer knows the story behind some of the shots requested.

Inform guests of any photos requiring their involvement – once you know which guests are going to star in your group images, do let them know in advance and if possible inform them of when these shots will take place. This avoids them rushing off to the reception venue or heading straight to the bar when they should be smiling beautifully in a group photo. It also prevents surprises on the day and cries of "Oh I don't want to be in this one – do I have to?". I always suggest that an usher or "vocally-gifted" member of the wedding party helps to round up friends and family for the groups shots and so informing them of this role before the day is also useful.

During the Preparations

Choose a room with space and light – if you have any control or choice over where you are getting ready and want some stunning preparation shots, look for a room with large windows or which is naturally bright and spacious. Small, dark, poky rooms can limit the look and variety of images that can be taken of you sprucing your hair up and donning your finest. Aside from the implications on the technical aspect of the photography, a dark room isn't the most uplifting and celebratory atmosphere for a wedding day and you will feel and look so much calmer and happy in a bright airy room.

Gather all the little details together – to save time and to become your photographer's favourite ever client (for one day at least – we're a fickle bunch), have all the little important details ready for when your photographer arrives; the flowers, the rings, the hip flask full of ·neat gin – whatever has been thought about and is special to you on your big day. It saves time and it helps your photographer to remember everything that plays a part in the narrative of your wedding.

Have a quick tidy before the photographer arrives – all photographers work differently, but most of the preparation photos are taken towards the end of the process and so it it not unusual for us to arrive to a scene of chaos and clutter. A little bit of wedding-related mess creates a sense of occasion but too much can be distracting in the images. A quick tidy-up before your photographer is due will be something they thank you for – trust me!

Factor in photo time – I always recommend that to get beautiful shots of you in your wedding attire (whether a dress, suit, kilt or polka dot bikini), be dressed and ready at least 30-45mins before your transport is arriving to collect you (if the ceremony is at another location) or the same amount of time before the start of the ceremony (if taking place at the same location). This is the minimum time needed to feel calm and relaxed and get the best possible images.

The Ceremony

Walk slowly – when walking down the aisle (and when walking through a confetti shower) walk nice and slowly. Savour the moment and take your time. It allows your photographer to get lots of fantastic images of you both. I know it can be a nerve-wracking time (especially on your way to the ceremony) but breathe deeply and try not rush these little journeys.

Keep your head up – as well as walking slowly, try to avoid looking at the floor. Talk to each other, make each other laugh, and / or smile at your guests because as beautiful as the top of your head may be, you can't beat seeing your happy faces in wedding photos!

Kiss Slowly – your first kiss and everyone is watching – get it over with quickly right? No! Once again slow down and enjoy it – make it count. A quick blink-and-you-miss-it peck on the cheek doesn't make for a great photograph so make the most of your first married kiss.

The Photo Session

Stay in one place for the group shots – it's tempting when you know everyone who should be in the next photo to wander off and look for them, but this wastes a lot of time. Stay put and let that aforementioned loudmouth do the donkey work. By staying put, you also ensure a consistent look to the group photos as you can remain in a central position throughout the set of images.

Ask what to do with spare limbs and body parts – if your photographer hasn't directed you and you feel a bit awkward, don't be afraid to ask what to do with your resting hand or arm. It might be that you look great just as you are, or that the photographer is simply sorting their settings before they pose you a little more. Either way it doesn't hurt to show that you are thinking about how you are looking and actively engaging in the shoot – be confident to say "Does my arm, leg, chin (insert relevant body part here) look OK?".

Don't feel guilty about not mingling with your guests – even those of you who want to invest a lot of time in getting some stunning photos may feel a bit bad about leaving poor Carol from the office being chatted up by boring Uncle Bob, but relax; everyone can cope without the newlyweds being in their eyesight at various points throughout the day. It's perfectly acceptable for you to be out and about having your photographs taken during certain moments of the day.

The Reception

Heads up for the speeches – aside from making sure the photographer knows when these are happening, make sure the photographer also knows if a particular surprise has been planned by any of the speakers so that they can be in the right place to capture the reactions of the married couple and their guests. However nervous you and your speakers are, try to remember to look up from your notes from time to time. It makes for a more interesting photo and keeps the audience a little more engaged.

Milk the first dance moment – yes another occasion when all eyes are on you so try not to spend the next 4 minutes looking directly down at the dance floor. Even if you are more of a wallflower than a wannabe Strictly champion, try to move a little around the dancefloor (or at the very least turn on the spot). It allows your photographer to get a wider variety of shots. Look into each others' eyes, have another kiss, and then smile – it's a magical moment.

After the Wedding

Share with friends and family – most photographers now provide a facility to share an online gallery of images and even allow guests to order prints and digital copies of their favourite photographs from the day. Some of you may happily allow your photographer to share some highlights across social media, but this is not something that every couple is happy with. However you decide to share your images with loved ones, try not to leave it until too long after the day; sharing your photos whilst the event is still fresh in their minds shows consideration and appreciation for the part they played in celebrating your marriage.

Of course, there are many many more hints, tips and tricks for improving the chances of getting fantastic images but hopefully these are enough to get you thinking about how your input can make a big difference.

As photographers, we don't expect you to remember all of these things and we will remind you when appropriate of how you can help us get great images of you and your loved ones. The main thing to remember is to be honest, open and involved in the photographic process. Photographs mean so much more when you feel you have played a huge role in the creation of them.

SUMMARY

- Be organised and honest. Plan your group shots and write a list of all the important details that you want your photographer to capture and inform them of any concerns or anxieties you have.

- Inform guests beforehand if they are going to to be part of the group photos – especially those who are not close family members and may not expect to be formally photographed. This avoids wasting time gently "persuading" begrudging guests to pose for the camera.

- Slow down at the key moments – when walking down the aisle, having your first kiss and swaying to your first dance song. Savour the moment and allow your photographer more time to get lots of awesome shots.

- Make your photographer aware of any surprises or changes to the running order so they are ready to capture these special moments.

12

After the Wedding

Congratulations! All those months of planning, preparing, and pulling your hair out are over. Your day was a huge success, tailored perfectly to fit your personality and values and regardless of any minor setbacks, slip-ups or moments of panic during the day you are now a happily married couple. This is when the real adventure and excitement begins.

In the first few days following a wedding you may be a little bit exhausted, a little bit deflated and – in some cases – a little bit sore headed! So what happens now? Well, the short answer is "enjoy the rest of your lives together" but that makes for a very short and uninformative chapter. So, before you drive off into the sunset in true Hollywood blockbuster style, here are just a few things that you can do to ease your transition from frenzied wedding-planners to never-been-happier newlyweds.

Relax

Whether the days following your wedding are spent in a Grade 1 Listed stately manor, on a sun-kissed golden-sanded beach, or in your parents' chintz–themed loft conversion; make sure you take some time to chill out and get some valuable couple time. Planning and executing your perfect wedding is no mean feat and whilst you may have had considerable help putting together your big day, you deserve some rest and recuperation and a huge pat on the back. Smugness is very much permitted at this stage and you are fully entitled to discuss the highlights from the day with each other (and various interested parties) for hours on end. Your status as centre-of-attention VIPs will all-too-quickly fade into obscurity so make the most of it whilst you still can!

Even if you aren't jetting off on your honeymoon immediately after the wedding, it is great to be able to spend some quality time together before real life kicks straight back in, and to take time to bask in that newly married glow; go on – it definitely suits you! A meal out, a trip to the cinema or even a pizza and a boxset provides a little bit of downtime and a chance to breathe again after the emotional roller-coaster that is your big day.

As previously mentioned, having a few exciting plans – whether in the days, the weeks or the months that follow – really help to eliminate the post-wedding blues. If you didn't find time to make these plans before the wedding, now is the perfect time to sit together and discuss all of the things you are excited about experiencing together and to firm up some plans and set some deadlines. Be specific and agree to prioritise some of these adventures before life gets in the way.

Sort Out the Paperwork

Yawn! No one likes admin, do they? Surprisingly, this is the bit you never seem to see in films or on TV. However, the sooner you start, the sooner you no longer have to think about it, so make sure you plan in a bit of time to sort out any necessary paperwork.

Following your wedding, one or both of you may have chosen to change your name and so this is usually the source of most of the necessary admin tasks. The process for officially changing your name is pretty straightforward and you can do some of this in advance of your wedding (including having your passport changed ready for your honeymoon) if you wish. You may want to take the same name as your partner, keep your own or amalgamate the two; the choice is yours. Whatever you choose, make sure you research what is needed for your name change to be legally recognised. Some changes require no more than the marriage certificate for the name change to be official, whilst others will require changing your name(s) via deed poll. As with all other aspects of your wedding and married life, go with what is right for both of you. Discuss the options beforehand and don't leave it until this moment to realise you cannot agree on how you will both be known from now on!

From your passport to your bank card, everything pertaining to your identity will need to be renamed in honour of your recent nuptials. A simple internet search can provide you with a checklist to use to tick off which companies and organisations you have successfully informed, and remind you of all the not-so-obvious people that you need to contact (this is where being a professional store card hoarder is not an advantage).

Don't Forget to Say Thanks

If, after reading this book, you decide what you really want to do is to elope to Gretna Green to say your vows far away from everyone you know and love, the chances are there might not be too many Thank You cards to write. However, for most people, wedding-planning has been a team effort and so, as soon as possible, show gratitude for those who helped you both before and / or during the day. Whether family members, friends, or the professionals that you hired to make your day truly unique; if you didn't make a point of thanking them on the day itself (and even if you did), handwriting Thank You notes is not only good from an etiquette point of view, but also provides another opportunity to remember all of the day's highlights and realise just how much love and support you both have around you.

Suppliers and friends love to feel appreciated so a little note can go a long way. Take an extra couple of minutes to state specifically what you are grateful for or how their input impacted your day. *"Thank you so much for being patient when the flower girls were getting upset – it really kept everyone relaxed and calm"* is far more genuine and meaningful than a generic mass-printed *"Thanks for being part of our day"* card or, worse still, an email.

A nice touch is to use a photo from your photographer – whether from your engagement shoot or the day itself – to use as the cover of your card. Some photographers will offer these as part of your photography package so check this when you book them.

Of course, all of your guests (not just those who played a part in the wedding planning) deserve a thank you too, so that's quite a few more cards to write, and once again, if gifts were given, make sure to mention their specific gift in your Thank You notes to show how much you value their thoughtfulness and generosity.

Write Some Reviews

Just as reviews are a great tool for selecting suppliers that are a perfect match for you, they are also a great way for us wedding professionals to get our name and business known to more couples, and enable us to help even more like-minded clients to have their own perfect wedding. Two or three sentences on your suppliers' online profiles can really make a huge difference not just to the suppliers themselves, but also to other couples who are now searching for their own team of brilliant wedding professionals.

I love reading reviews from happy couples and it's great that words and phrases such as "stress-free", "patient" and "calm" seem to be common throughout my reviews. It helps to know that I am doing my job well and that all the little extra effort and time I invest in my couples are noticed and appreciated. Constructive criticism can also help us to improve the products and customer service we deliver to couples in the future.

Never underestimate how thrilled we are to receive a glowing review from a happy couple. I usually do a little dance around my office after reading a lovely write-up from a client; so if the thought of that isn't too disturbing, jot down a few lines to tell the world how fab you think your suppliers are.

Be Patient...and then Prompt...with Your Wedding Photos

Hopefully, you will have agreed a set time frame with your photographer for the turnaround of your wedding photos. As excited as you will be to see them all and relive the day, try to avoid pestering your photographer for your images unless the agreed timeframe has now passed.

If your photography package included an album or, upon seeing your images, you decide that they are too special not to be presented in such a way, then try to make your photo selections as soon as possible so that your photographer has plenty of time to design and order your album. Some album suppliers also take longer than others to process and deliver orders, so the sooner you choose your favourites, the sooner your coffee table can be adorned with your beautiful wedding photographs.

Two to three weeks after delivering wedding images to a couple (possibly my favourite part of my job), I always factor in a little time for the design and ordering of an album. Designing an album in a way that expertly narrates the story of your special day is much easier when it is fresh in my memory and when the images have recently been edited. Whilst you are perfectly within your rights to order an album 6 months or a year down the line, remember how many weddings your photographer will have photographed since then. They will now have to find the time to re-familiarise themselves with your wedding images to design and order your album, when this time may already be allocated to meeting with couples who, (just as you once were), are excitedly planning their big day and desperately need their expert help and advice.

I know that choosing your favourite images from a collection of hundreds is challenging and time-consuming but try not to put it off; not only will the album be something to look forward to and enjoy, but the process of making your choices is a lovely activity to do together as newlyweds (and definitely beats arguing over whose turn it is to put the bins out).

Finally...

Apply the Themes of This Book to Your Married Life Together

As the title of this book suggests, I am passionate about couples being able to express their own individuality and embrace all of the wonderful things that make them unique; not just during the wedding planning process but also throughout their day-to-day life as a married couple.

Many of the underlying principles outlined in this book can be applied to life in general; feeling comfortable in our own skin and not comparing ourselves to others, not following fads or trends, and ignoring the pressure to act or look how society expects us to. You have found someone who loves you exactly as you are and wants to spend the rest of their life with you. Let this beautiful fact remind you that there is no need to be anyone other than yourself.

Learn to listen and take advice from those who love and support you and genuinely want the best for you, but try to recognise the difference between these people and those who simply want to force their own ideas and agendas on you. It is possible to be open-minded and always open to new ideas and perspectives, whilst at the same time have a strong sense of self and know your own mind. Taking time to identify our own values and beliefs and constantly reflecting on what is important to us can help us to make difficult choices at all stages throughout our lives and enable us to stand up for what we feel is right, even when faced with criticism and cynicism.

Collaborating with like-minded individuals – whether during the wedding planning process, at work or in our social life – is a fantastic way to achieve our goals, increase our confidence and make changes in our own and other people's lives for the better. If you have successfully coordinated photographers, florists, venue managers, dressmakers and caterers (and you will have by this point), you are capable of working with a diverse range of individuals from all walks of life to accomplish incredible things. Just imagine what else you can achieve using your powers of coordination and collaboration!

Never apologise for being who you are, loving who you love or for being 100% unique. Don't dare to be different, dare to be yourself.

Have a wonderful wedded life together.

Summary

- Plan time to rest and relax after the big day – especially if you are not immediately going on your honeymoon. A day or two to catch your breath and bask in your newlywed glow is great for the mind, body and soul.

- Send Thank You cards or letters to all those who have helped make your day a success. Handwritten notes mean a lot more than a quick generic email.

- Spend a little time reviewing your suppliers so that that couples who are now planning their wedding will be able to find their own perfect vendors.

- As a married couple, continue to celebrate your unique qualities, be proud of the love you have found and dare to be yourself throughout all of your future endeavours.

Acknowledgements

Thank you to all the wonderful clients and wedding suppliers that I have had the pleasure of working with thus far in my career and all my clients who have booked me for their upcoming weddings. Working with you all makes my job the best in the world. Extra special thanks to those of you who were happy for your photographs to be featured in this book.

Thanks to the friendly and ever-helpful team at YouCaxton for your advice and expert knowledge.

A massive thank you to Gill Tiney for your unwavering support, inspiration and motivation. You have held up a mirror to my potential and made me realise how much I have to offer the world.

Finally, thank you James for always believing in me, unconditionally loving me and continually providing me with the happiest memories a man could ever wish for. Never forget how extraordinary you are.

About the Author

Ross Willsher is a professional wedding and portrait photographer who specialises in celebrating love in all its forms. Having previously studied Photo Imaging at Morley College in London, Ross is a firm believer in valuing everyone's unique qualities and capturing their individuality through natural, relaxed and stress-free photography. Originally from the Cotswolds, Ross loves incorporating the natural environment into his photographs and loves how the great outdoors can enable people to feel calm and comfortable in their own skin.

A proud uncle and wannabe "Star Baker", Ross spends his free time being creative (and messy) in the kitchen and listening to songs that either soothe, energise or inspire the soul.

He lives in Chelmsford, Essex, with James – his partner of 10 years – and his work takes him across London and throughout the UK.

To see more of Ross' work and for more information relating to the topics discussed in the book please visit

www.rosswillsherphotography.co.uk

You can contact Ross by emailing

info@rosswillsherphotography.co.uk